QUEER TASTES

UNCONVENTIONAL REPRESENTATION IN HORROR FILMS

CAT VOLEUR

Published by
Agita Publishing (formerly From Beyond Press) | Chicago, IL
agitapublishing.com
mike@agitapublishing.com
Instagram @agita.publishing, Bluesky @agitapublishing.bsky.social

ISBN: 979-8-9925941-4-0
Library of Congress Control Number: 2026944026

TABLE OF CONTENTS

A GENTLE WARNING TO READERS

Each essay includes a summary,
but this book is written with the presumption
that you have seen
(or do not plan to see) the movies.
Spoilers abound. Proceed with caution.

THE
IMPORTANCE
OF IMPERFECTION

There is a glorious thing that happens in films when a director commits a piece of themselves to the screen. Each person in the audience may view what they're seeing differently. Some may be offended or appalled. It may toss fuel onto the fires of hate and intolerance. That same movie could, in that same moment, inspire understanding and connection.

Art should be a conversation, always. I find this to be especially true for a medium as subjective as cinema and in a genre as transgressive as horror. The conversations can become heated, messy, or unpleasant, but that does not make them less worthy of having.

In *Queer Tastes*, I argue that the viewer who finds beauty in an ugly film is just as valid in their experience as the dozens of people who took offense. This is true of any community, any genre, and any one weirdo—but I am not covering all of that here. The examples I'm bringing to the table for this book are horror movies, the LGBTQIA+ community, and myself. I am that one weirdo.

This is, in many ways, my story.

The essays ahead detail my experience in the queer community and my struggles to fit in. They tie in very closely to my media tastes, because as a massive fan of this genre, I have always discovered the most about myself when cinema has inspired me to look at the world in a new light.

I struggled a lot with this before I found where I fit in. When my friends were of an age to come out, I was still just watching horror movies. I mostly dated guys who also watched horror movies. As my queer friends got older and more confident in their own tastes,

I noticed that they liked horror movies that were very different to the ones I liked. This made me feel, more than any self-identifiers, that I did not fully fit in with them.

I was straight-passing by circumstance and believed it into my early twenties, even when I found out I had kissed more girls than my partner had at the time. I didn't think I could be gay. I was living with a guy, we were in love, and most importantly, I didn't like the things that my gay friends liked.

Horror helped me realize that I could fool my friends, and I could fool my partner, but I was very tired of fooling myself. I didn't have to be like my queer friends just because I too was queer. I wish I'd known sooner. I wish I'd seen myself reflected not just in the genre, but in the specific subgenres of movies that I'd loved.

I pitched this book as a collection of essays about the unsung heroes of queer horror films. The hated ones. The controversial ones. The problematic and highly debated ones. I wanted to recommend movies that I never saw on other Pride lists. This whole project was supposed to be an angry declaration of "why not these?"

When the book was picked up and I embarked on the heavier research for it, I realized there actually are valid arguments about why some of my favorites are not well-respected or loved in the community. Some are overwhelmingly triggering. Some perpetuate harmful stereotypes. One was blamed for an uptick in hate crimes, though I was unable to find substantial evidence of that being true.

I started including that research in my notes, as well as counterpoints to my own opinions. My rough draft quickly spiraled out and became messy. I began to once again experience that feeling of "otherness" that had made me feel so isolated from my community. I almost scrapped the entire book because of my pain over loving the things I'm "not supposed" to love.

It was my very patient editor who suggested that I open up more. He suggested that I share more personal opinions with fewer caveats, and that I have confidence in my lived experiences.

He reminded me of my own goal with this project, which was to embrace the nonconformity. I said from the beginning that this book was for the problematic and the imperfect, and that I wanted those misfits within our ranks to feel less alone.

It was scary to make that shift. I had pitched this as an objective research project, and had never envisioned it being quite as personal as it got while working on it. I'd not fully considered the vulnerability involved in publishing and standing behind my most problematic takes.

But here's the thing.

The twenty movie recommendations in this book are personal. They were an intimate part of my queer journey and my eventual acceptance of myself. These are the films that made me question myself and my worldviews and my preferences. They are still teaching me things about my identity because I've spent the last year studying them and learning about my place in our history. I have read and watched and interacted with so many other queer creators during the writing of this book. That is all thanks to the unhinged list of recommendations that I'm about to share with you.

If you like the problematic, extreme, disgusting movies that ruffle feathers, please know that you are not alone. You're not a worse queer person, or a worse ally, or even a worse human for loving films that others turn their backs on.

If you don't already like these movies, then consider this your invitation to step into my skin for a while. See what I see. Understand the good that a film can do—even when the same film is doing bad. Remember while you are here that beauty is in the eye of the beholder, and let me lend you my eyes.

REBECCA (1940)

SETTING THE STAGE FOR SAPPHIC SUBTEXT

"But what goes on in the twisted,
torturous minds of women
would baffle anyone."

—Daphne du Maurier, *Rebecca*

Vital Statistics

Directed by Alfred Hitchcock
Written by Robert E. Sherwood and Joan Harrison
Cinematography by George Barnes
Edited by Hal C. Kern and James E. Newcome
Starring Laurence Olivier as Maxim de Winter, Joan Fontaine
as Mrs. de Winter, Judith Anderson as Mrs. Danvers, and
George Sanders as Jack Favell
1940, USA, 130 min.

et us first address the elephant in the room: it is not exactly groundbreaking to cite *Rebecca* as a fairly early piece of LGBTQIA+ horror cinema. Though queer themes can be spotted in adaptations that were coming out as early as the 1910s, those were (by necessity) silent films and open to more interpretation as a result of the medium. *The Picture of Dorian Gray* by Oscar Wilde saw a handful of screen adaptations in that era that played with the book's queer subtext. One of the earliest and most iconic horror films was the 1922 *Dracula* adaptation *Nosferatu*, directed by F. W. Murnau, whose identity as a gay man certainly played into his reading of Bram Stoker's original text.

In my initial conception of this project, I had hoped to keep my focus exclusively on the unsung and underrated titles—hidden gems whose queer themes were underappreciated. I began by listing my favorites, my hot takes, and the movies that had made me feel most seen throughout my personal journey. I quickly discovered that this only got me as far back as the 1970s and left out many staples of the genre that might otherwise have provided important context to the state of representation.

Trying to scrape up films that I recommend that hadn't been picked clean for commentary stopped feeling feasible around the 1960s. Creature features were still running rampant through this period, and for reasons that I'll get into later, it felt very important to the nature of my project that I avoid recommending them here.

Another big issue, of course, is that the further back I looked, the more coverage even obscure or loosely coded Pride films already had. Queer writers, critics, filmmakers, and essayists have been covering the topic of representation longer than I've been alive. Going so far back, especially to a time when the Hays Code[1] of censorship restricted how queerness could be depicted, left me barren of any fresh titles to bring to your attention.

At this point I had to go back to the drawing board and open up the parameters of my full recommendations list. I'm grateful that it happened so early on in my process because it made me stop and reconsider the cohesiveness of what I was trying to put together.

One thing that you'll notice as you work your way through this book is that as the movies become more modern, they become more niche, and my opinions become more controversial. I consider myself quite lucky to be living in a time where an individual can be so discerning about what media they feel represents them. We have so many options for queer horror we can gravitate toward. This was not always the case for audiences in, say, 1940.

Rather than starting my list in the 1970s, or forcing myself to ponder an era of silent films that didn't personally inform my own identity, I decided to start my list with the classics I feel best represent the themes and styles that you can still see reflected in my modern picks. I kept my core group of movies I already intended to passionately recommend, and then chose a few earlier examples of films that I felt paved the way for those favorites, stood the test of time, and forged my personal tastes.

Enter *Rebecca*.

This 1940 Alfred Hitchcock classic is an adaptation of Daphne du Maurier's 1938 gothic novel of the same name. Both stories follow Mrs. de Winter after her whirlwind romance to

---

1. The Hays Code (more formally known as The Motion Picture Production Code) was a set of guidelines drafted by Will H. Hays that imposed limits on what could and could not be shown onscreen in a Hollywood film. The code was active from 1934 to 1968 and drastically limited how homosexual relationships could be depicted during this time.

Mr. de Winter, and how she is plagued by the lingering presence of his first wife: Rebecca. Rebecca's absence is a character unto itself—sometimes a stronger character than Mrs. de Winter, who never receives so much as a first name. She feels utterly lost in her new home at Manderley, and in perpetual competition with a dead woman whom she has never even met.

The film was well received, and was Hitchcock's only Best Picture winner, despite being the first Hollywood movie he ever directed. Critics called it "haunting" and "romantic." The adaptation is more subtle in its sapphic themes, in no small part because of the switch of medium from page to screen. The paranoia and obsession were omnipresent in Mrs. de Winter's narration of the book, whereas Hitchcock had to rely more on atmosphere and visual cues in his approach to the story—which is not to say that the queer themes were completely absent onscreen.

In fact, a prime target for queer cinephile analysis was Mrs. Danvers, played by Judith Anderson, who was quite faithful to her literary counterpart. She is, if you will pardon a sweeping generalization, the Renfield to Rebecca's Dracula. Out of loyalty to Rebecca, she humiliates and belittles the new Mrs. de Winter, but the passion behind her cruelties has left many audiences questioning the nature of their relationship.

"You thought you could be Mrs. de Winter, live in her house, walk in her steps, take the things that were hers! But she's too strong for you. You can't fight her—no one ever got the better of her. Never, never."

In the book, Mrs. Danvers's obsession with Rebecca, and its causes, were left open to interpretation by the reader. Judith Anderson's passionate portrayal of the character brings such questions to a fever pitch in the film. Is it love that keeps her so loyal to the ghost of a woman she had once served?

A logical extension of that discussion has been whether or not Rebecca herself was bisexual. It's a topic that, of course, was never addressed onscreen, but many essays and op-eds have raised it over the years. A more straightforward and literal interpretation of their relationship in the film is that Rebecca, prone to scheming and theatrics, welcomed any and all attention regardless of romantic subtext. While I find the possibility that Rebecca was an early queer-coded villain of sorts, this actually has little to do with why the story resonated for me personally, and why I chose it to open my recommendations list.

This entire era of cinema relies so heavily on context that I found it best to begin with a film that, while generally accepted as a piece of LGBTQIA+ friendly media, hinges entirely on the viewer's interpretation. It's also one of the strongest early examples of a theme that you'll find recurring throughout my upcoming recommendations: obsession as a sort of intimacy.

Mrs. Danvers is openly infatuated with Rebecca, and the fact that she frames those feelings as positive has opened them up to sexual or romantic interpretation throughout the years. I would argue that the new Mrs. de Winter is just as obsessed—if not more so—with her predecessor at Manderley.

There are so many stories of women who are obsessed with becoming like or positioning themselves in competition with other women before eventually coming out of the closet. It has gotten to be somewhat of a trope. We see it with celebrities, and fictional characters, and I know it's something I have personally experienced. Society pits women against each other so often that same-sex feelings of attraction can easily be warped or misinterpreted.

Mrs. de Winter frames her increasing paranoia about Rebecca's lingering presence as a fear that she won't measure up, or be able to satisfy her husband. The more obsessed she becomes with the idea of his first wife, the less her actions appear to be motivated by the attention of a man at all. Mrs. de Winter wishes to emulate someone whom she imagines as being perfect in every way, but whose approval she'll never be able to have.

This was the queer aspect of the film that most resonated with my experience. Before I knew what it meant to be attracted to other women, I spent a lot of time feeling jealous or even resentful of women whom I perceived as more desirable than myself. It never occurred to me that I may just desire them.

Obsession, subtext, and unrequited longing are all integral to my queer tastes in horror media. There are few movies in the world that encapsulate those themes so entirely as *Rebecca*.

LES DIABOLIQUES
(1955)
LEAVE IT
TO THE
FRENCH

"I may be reactionary, but this is absolutely astounding—the legal wife consoling the mistress! No, no, and no!"

—Un professeur, *Les Diaboliques*

Vital Statistics

Directed by Henri-Georges Clouzot
Written by Henri-Georges Clouzot and Jérôme Géronimi
Cinematography by Armand Thirard
Edited by Madeleine Gug
Starring Simone Signoret as Nicole Horner, Véra Clouzot as Christina Delasalle, and Paul Meurisse as Michel Delasalle
1955, France, 117 min.

ollowing *Rebecca* we have another very sapphic film: *Les Diaboliques*. It was also inspired by a book, this one entitled *Celle qui n'était plus* (or in the English translation, *She Who Was No More*) written by Pierre Boileau and Thomas Narcejac. This was very nearly another Hitchcock film, but he was beaten to the adaptation rights by Henri-Georges Clouzot. It is a common misconception in review circles that the book served as inspiration for Hitchcock's 1958 film *Vertigo*, but in fact that was a book of the same name also written by Boileau-Narcejac.

Compared to *Rebecca*, the sapphic themes felt very explicit in the movie, and especially in the book. While *Les Diaboliques* stands on its own as a piece of queer horror history, I am particularly fascinated with its largely unsuccessful attempts at making the screen version feel more heterosexual.

The movie follows the wife and mistress of cruel headmaster Michel Delassalle, who have teamed up to murder him. Wife Christina and mistress Nicole drown him in the city to establish their alibi before smuggling the body back into the boarding school he runs to be discovered after the break. Tension builds as they await news of the body being discovered, which does not come. Michel's body goes missing, and Christina begins to believe that she is being haunted by the husband she killed. This is bad for her heart condition, and her desire to turn herself in to the law is initially hampered only by her close relationship to Nicole.

The twist that shocked audiences back in 1955 was that Michel wasn't dead at all. He and Nicole had conspired to fake his drowning, then the disappearance of his body and the haunting, to try to scare Christina to death so they could be together and live off her family money.

On paper, this should be more straight-passing than the original text. In the book, Fernand's mistress, Lucienne, convinces him to take out an insurance policy with his wife, Mireille. She fakes Mireille's drowning and the two women team up to drive Fernand into a suicidal madness before splitting the insurance payout between themselves.

There are a few aspects where the movie does seem less blatantly queer. The biggest difference, obviously, is that the two women don't end up together. (It's important to note that in the book's English translation, Lucienne and Mireille are described as "friends," but this term and their relationship both were more ambiguous in the original French text.) Another key difference is that the husband is not the narrator in the film the way he was in the book. Through that shift, we lose a lot of the classically lesbian traits that he describes his mistress as having. "Strange how little feminine she was. Even when they made love . . . How had she ever become his mistress?"

Finally, there is the added context of him being an abuser in the film, which gives Christina a more pressing motivation than wishing to run away with her "friend."

In other ways, though, the women's relationship seems far more overtly queer in the movie. Since the true intention of the scheme isn't revealed until the end, most of the runtime follows Nicole and Christina comforting one another. The chemistry between their respective actresses, Simone Signoret and Véra Clouzot, is undeniable. Since Michel is portrayed as an abuser, neither one of the women ever have a scene with him where the audience roots for their relationship—which some could argue made the ending fall comparatively flat.

Though it lacks the same sapphic framing as its source

material, *Les Diaboliques* masquerades quite successfully for over an hour and a half as a story of two women putting one another above a man. This is confirmed through actions, words, and touches throughout the movie. There is one scene in particular where they have lured Michel out to Nicole's apartment and he asks Christina if they are lying in her bed there or Nicole's. In a blink-and-you-miss-it line, she answers "ours."

Now, one of the big reasons I wished to include this movie on my list is that I love it. It's one of the first movies I was able to identify queer subtext in at all, and I have no doubt that it was formative in shaping my preferences—both as a woman attracted to other women, and as a fan of the psychological horror genre.

Something else that I wanted to highlight as early as possible which is strongly embodied by this pick is the French approach to storytelling. This will come back later with my love of the New French Extremity movement in horror, but it also affected my early views on relationships and story structure. To this day, I still gravitate toward more unconventional dynamics between characters and more convoluted conclusions.

French films often have a strong focus on sexuality and tragedy. They portray such things as important, sometimes glamorous, but ultimately inevitable. There is something so human and relatable in these aspects of their storytelling that I find French horror to be very grounded and realistic even when it takes on fantastical proportions.

Finally, what appeals to me so much about *Les Diaboliques* is that it is a horror film, first and foremost. This will be another recurring theme through my list, and something it is best to understand about my preferences early. A movie could check all of the representation boxes and I don't think I'd give a single damn if it wasn't first engaging. All of these picks, and *Les Diaboliques* in particular, are movies that I would recommend to my straight friends just as quickly as I would recommend them to my queer friends. There is an added element of interest because of the way that the relationship between Nicole and Christine so easily invites questions, but my love stems from the ever-mounting terror that Clouzot delivered in this adaptation.

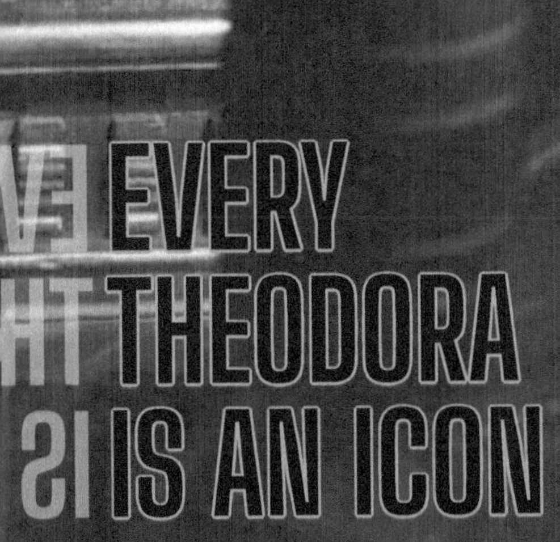
THE HAUNTING
(1963)
EVERY
THEODORA
IS AN ICON

"Duty and conscience were, for Theodora, attributes which belonged properly to Girl Scouts."

—Shirley Jackson,
The Haunting of Hill House

Vital Statistics

Directed by Robert Wise
Written by Nelson Gidding
Cinematography by Davis Boulton
Edited by Ernest Walter
Starring Julie Harris as Eleanor Lance, Claire Bloom as Theodora, Richard Johnson as Dr. John Markway, and Russ Tamblyn as Luke Sannerson
1963, USA/UK, 114 min.

My first two recommendations were about establishing the roots of queer themes that still resonate today, as well as setting the stage of cultural repression so that we can watch it come into focus over the decades. I recommend *The Haunting* for a much simpler reason: Theodora.

Yes, there are feelings of otherness, exclusion, and longing that are wrapped up in the core of the narrative. This is true of both Robert Wise's film and its source material, Shirley Jackson's 1959 novel *The Haunting of Hill House*. One could argue that the nature of the story is inherently queer-coded, but no one has to make that case because Theodora is such a beloved sapphic icon.

The movie is about Dr. John Markway, who is trying to study the paranormal energies he believes to be present at the ninety-year-old mansion known as Hill House. He invites guests to participate in the study by staying in the house and remarking on any strange experiences they have. The only people to accept the invitation are Luke (the heir to the mansion), Eleanor (who had a paranormal encounter as a child), and our dear psychic, Theodora.

A more popular iteration of this character (and admittedly my personal favorite) is Kate Siegel's portrayal of Theodora Crain in Mike Flanagan's 2018 Netflix adaptation, *The Haunting of Hill House*. In the limited series we are treated to more time with the character. This means we get to see her interact with other women, have conversations about her sexuality, and explore her family's reaction to her coming out. There's even a lesbian scene so steamy and explicit that even conceiving of putting it onscreen in the 1960s would have been unthinkable. Truly, we are living in a blessed time.

None of this would have been possible, however, without Claire Bloom's portrayal of Theodora in *The Haunting*. This was the sort of role that was groundbreaking for the community at the time. Not only is Theodora a lesbian, but being a lesbian is far from the most interesting thing about her. She's mysterious and poised, and her sexuality is treated as neither a red flag nor a joke. Though it was slowly becoming more common to see homosexuality mentioned, it was practically unheard of to see it brought to life in a way that wasn't caricatured or deeply harmful.

While Theodora's sexuality is not a strong focus in the film, an early version of Nelson Gidding's script showed her breaking up with her girlfriend prior to her arrival at Hill House. Robert Wise ultimately decided to take a subtler route with her—likely a good decision, as her character's inclusion was already a fight he had to take up with censors.

Bloom supported the change in interviews at the time, and expressed her admiration for Wise's decision. "At first I was disappointed, but when I saw the film itself, I realized how correct he was." Years later, in a career retrospective interview with the British Film Institute, she once again brought up the importance of those deleted scenes. "The character's lesbianism was made more obvious in the original script...but I know that the film is highly appreciated."

There is something particularly heartwarming to me that not only was *The Haunting* a massive step forward in representation in horror, but that the team behind it was so intentional in their approach. They set a high standard by deciding first what would make the best movie, and only then considering what aspects they could get past censors, an ongoing battle for Wise after production. The Hays Office demanded additional cuts before allowing the studio to release the film and put specific restrictions on the character. They did not want to see Theo touching Eleanor at any point, a rule that's broken several times throughout the final product.

I love every version of Theodora, from her glamorous appearance in Jackson's original text all the way to Siegel's more overt portrayal in the 2018 version. I even loved Catherine Zeta-Jones as Theodora even though the 1999 version of *The Haunting* is lacking in most other respects. Every Theodora is a queer icon in her own right, but none paved the way for the character's acceptance as Claire Bloom did.

THE TEXAS CHAIN SAW MASSACRE (1974)

SATIRE, GENDER ROLES, AND AESTHETICS

"It's a hard movie to watch—a hard movie to rewatch—and yet I keep coming back because it's worth it."

—Karyn Kusama, *Chain Reactions*

Vital Statistics

Directed by Tobe Hooper
Written by Kim Henkel and Tobe Hooper
Cinematography by Daniel Pearl
Edited by Sallye Richardson and Larry Carroll
Starring Marilyn Burns as Sally Hardesty, Gunnar Hansen as Leatherface, and Paul A. Pertain as Franklin Hardesty
1974, USA, 83 min.

When you think about great LGBTQ+ movies, you probably don't think about Tobe Hooper and Kim Henkel's horror classic, *The Texas Chain Saw*[2] *Massacre*. But why?

Since this is one of my early unpopular opinions, I will refrain from calling Leatherface a queer icon, but I don't think it's a stretch to interpret him as genderqueer in some capacity. I believe, at a bare minimum, this film deserves to be part of the conversation about onscreen crossdressing in much the same way Hitchcock's *Psycho* gets worked in.

It used to ruffle my feathers to see Norman Bates offered as potential representation for the actions he committed as his mother persona because it felt like one of the genre's most blatant examples of conflating gender identity with mental illness. However, after many years, much research, and some context about Anthony Perkins's journey with his sexuality, I became more sympathetic to Bates's inclusion. After all, the core concept of this project is that it's not about the purity of the

---

2. In the opening text crawl of the film, the events depicted are described as "The Texas Chain Saw Massacre" with "chain" and "saw" as separate words. On the cover of the movie and in promotional materials, "chainsaw" is one word. When the original 1974 movie is discussed in print, or listed on review sites such as Rotten Tomatoes or IMDb it's almost always presented as two words. However, the franchise at large, and the other franchise installments, favor the one word "chainsaw." This was absolutely infuriating to try and get to the bottom of, and now I pass the information along to you.

representation; it's about what viewers can get out of engaging with it.

In much the same spirit, and with the hope to expand the list of classics that get recommended for Pride Month, I would like to offer a closer examination of one of my favorites. I have a theory as to why it may have been left by the wayside, but first let me make my case for its inclusion.

The Texas Chain Saw Massacre follows Sally Hardesty, her brother, her boyfriend, and two other friends, roadtripping to make sure that her grandfather's body has not been exhumed in a series of grave robberies and corpse mutilations being reported in the area. After encountering a creepy hitchhiker, they find themselves at the mercy of a cannibalistic family of murderers, being picked off one by one. This includes Leatherface, who later became known as one of the genre's great slashers, headlining one of the biggest and longest running horror franchises.

Leatherface gets explored more in the sequels, along with his family and the entire mythology, but the original film was pretty bare bones. (No cannibalism pun intended.) How you wish to perceive his actions in it is probably colored by which sequels you prefer and how many you consider to be part of the canon. Like any franchise spanning nine films, there are multiple timeline resets, installments that the fanbase chooses to ignore, and widely accepted theories. There is one scene in particular that I want to center this conversation around, however.

Toward the end of the movie, Sally is a captive guest at the family's dinner table. The tension in this scene is built between Sally's screaming as she takes in one horror after another and the ritual of what the family perceives as a wholesome dinner together. Leatherface is not only wearing a mask made of a human face, but has applied makeup and a wig to it. I struggle to find an interpretation of Leatherface's presentation at this event that doesn't paint him, or his family, in a queer light to some degree.

Leatherface's role within his family sees him take on more

domestic tasks throughout the entire film—jobs that would be considered feminine within the patriarchal unit that is being satirized. He prepares food, he decorates, he tends to the elderly, and we now have this scene where he is making himself look pretty. A cruel reading of these events is that this is something thrust upon him by the others, which would make it look more like abuse than gender expression. Even this more cynical view has a place in this discussion. Being forced to conform to your family's preconceived notions about your place at their table is one of the most classic queer struggles in media.

However, I prefer an interpretation that paints the family in a warmer light: maybe this is how Leatherface feels most comfortable. Because he is a nonverbal character, we don't get deep into his thoughts or feelings about his role or his sense of self-expression. We are left to draw our own conclusions about how he sees himself and his contributions within the household. The idea that he's drawn to roles more traditionally held by women could leave the door open for an imagining of his identity where Leatherface is trans or genderfluid or even just a willing participant in crossdressing—all things that fall under the larger umbrella term of queer.

A common "wishlist" item in queer spaces is that people want to see more supportive families depicted for queer characters. While I recognize the absurdity of calling an abusive family of murderous cannibals a good support system, I think this particular line of logic about his presentation offers some nuance in that regard. He's being yelled at and swatted by the family, but he's not being outcast for the role he's taken on. He doesn't even seem forced to choose a gender role because while two of his three faces are of women, he also wears the more traditionally masculine tuxedo to complete the look.

I mentioned earlier how difficult it was to find horror films that weren't already picked clean for discussion. Given how many parallels to queer narratives there are in the film, I found myself surprised to realize just how seldom this one gets brought up in that context. I am not the first person to ever point it out. I am just one of the loudest and most passionate.

Why is that?

Circling back to why I believe this film has been left by the wayside of gay culture, it might very well come down to aesthetics.

The Texas Chain Saw Massacre is one of the dirtiest, grimiest, most unsettling things I've ever seen. The sets are unclean, the world looks dilapidated, you can practically smell the blood as you watch. It's a movie that a lot of casual horror fans will only watch once, and that any viewer is unlikely to forget.

I would once more bring *Psycho* up as a point of comparison. It is a polished piece of art with gorgeous, standard-setting cinematography and absolutely iconic visuals. Hitchcock was a legend, and this piece of his in particular is loved by cinephiles and horrorhounds alike. You can catch a lot of flak in many circles for not liking *Psycho*, and I wonder if that hasn't made it a safer film to gravitate toward.

There are many "safe" movies that the queer community at large has embraced, or that carry enough weight with critics that it feels understandable to wish to see yourself in them. *The Texas Chain Saw Massacre* is interesting to look at as a potentially queer horror film because while it has retroactively been embraced as a foundational horror movie, it was not initially well received.

Joe Bob Briggs, who describes *The Texas Chain Saw Massacre* as the greatest movie ever made, also described it as "a movie whose very title became America's cultural shorthand for perversity, moral decline, and especially the corruption of children."[3] The movie had to be recut to avoid an X rating by the Motion Picture Association of America, and even the R-rated version was widely banned abroad.

It also essentially killed the career of its lead actress, Marilyn Burns. While she has gone down in horror history as the original final girl, studios would forever associate her with the movie,

---

3. *The Last Drive-In,* "Dinners of Death," 2018.

which greatly tarnished her reputation as an actress. Many of the actors regretted their involvement because of the film's reputation for being vulgar and sadistic.

Hooper oversaw editors Sallye Richardson and Larry Caroll for eight months to turn the footage into what we can acknowledge today as a masterpiece. The countless quick cuts make it feel like we've seen something truly harrowing, even as the actual blood is kept to a minimum. Your imagination wants to fill in those gaps, making it more effective than any prosthetics might have been.

It is understandable, perhaps, why a community that's already ostracized might not wish to hold up something so grotesque as representational for them.

I discovered my passion for the horror genre during the "torture porn" era of the early 2000s, which I do believe shaped my tastes greatly. This informs several of my upcoming recommendations, but also in a broader sense, helps explain my preference for grittier, grimier aesthetics. *The Texas Chain Saw Massacre* has always been one of my favorite classics (and indeed, one of my favorite films) because it laid the groundwork for so many of the first scary movies that I ever got to experience on the big screen. *Saw* and *Hostel* and I think even *Final Destination* wouldn't have been possible if Hooper hadn't pushed boundaries with this piece.

This movie screams horror to me, in every sense of the word. As a horror fan, I always recommend it to anyone interested in the genre and its roots. As a member of the LGBTQ+ community, I wonder if I wouldn't have found my place earlier if I'd seen Leatherface in more queer discussions. If members of the community I looked up to had recommended more of those unsettling aesthetics that I find myself so drawn to, perhaps I could have spent less time as the token straight friend.

SUSPIRIA
(1977)
THE
SURREAL
BEAUTY
OF DEATH

"Women, girls, are very important in my movies because I remember how my mother depicted them, how she elevated them."

—Dario Argento, *Dario Argento Panico*

Vital Statistics

Directed by Dario Argento
Written by Dario Argento and Daria Nicolodi
Cinematography by Luciano Tovoli
Edited by Franco Fraticelli
Starring Jessica Harper as Suzy Bannion, Stefania Casini as Sara Simms, and Barbara Magnolfi as Olga Ivanova
1977, Italy, 99 min.

n the last chapter, I spoke about how a film's aesthetics can push away viewers. In this chapter, I want to talk about how they can draw in an audience, and make even the most abstract stories resonate.

Suspiria was an important movie in my journey because for a long time it was one of the only horror movies that felt like common ground between myself and my friends in the queer community. I mentioned in the introduction how much I struggled with that feeling of disconnect, and while *Suspiria* was not single-handedly enough to bridge that gap in my mind, it gave us something to talk about that wasn't just vampires or werewolves. It was something that could tide me over until I found my place and my voice.

The movie follows dancer Suzy Bannion, who has been accepted into Freiburg, a prestigious German ballet academy. Immediately upon her arrival, and in the days that follow, the student population is beset by several horrific and unlikely deaths. While trying to get to the bottom of the strange goings on, Suzy discovers that Freiburg was founded to teach not only dance, but also the occult.

It is difficult to concisely describe the plot of *Suspiria*—but it is not the plot that matters half so much as the presentation. The deaths are shown through a lens that is more unflinching than in *The Texas Chain Saw Massacre*, but the violence is so beautifully lit and stylized that the effect is as magical and alluring as it is grotesque.

It was surprising to look back and acknowledge this as a foundational Pride movie for me, because the queer themes are as intangible and ethereal as the film itself. There is something to be said for the anecdotal evidence of simply noticing that a community gravitates toward a certain film, even without deep analysis. Taking a closer look at those patterns within your own circles is an important part of gauging your space and your tastes. In fact it's a simple exercise that I encourage you to engage in for yourself, even if you are the sort of person who doesn't want to pick apart every film you see for queer themes. For a long time, that was something I had very little interest in doing.

If a movie resonates with you, helps you on your journey, or teaches you about yourself, it is okay to embrace it as a part of your own, personal, queer canon. People do that all the time, especially when they are lacking in representation.

However, this is a book of essays, and I cannot simply chalk up my experience with *Suspiria* to "queer vibes" because that would make me a terrible essayist. So, aside from aesthetics, and the fact that my friends all appreciate this pick, what makes it a queer movie?

Part of that connection comes from my experience as a woman. Being a horror fan, and a horror fan with very specific tastes, I didn't get the chance to fall in love with horror media that felt as though it was made for women. In the 2024 documentary *Chain Reactions*, Alexandra Heller-Nicholas spoke of her experience being a young woman interested in *The Texas Chain Saw Massacre* and how she felt that those sorts of movies were "very gendered, and forbidden for little girls."

That was a point of contention between me and my parents, being a little girl who mostly loved the grittier horror films. Before I knew what *The Texas Chain Saw Massacre* was, and a few years before I was permitted to start seeing R-rated films in the theater, I felt like I was being kept from some of the most badass women in the genre.

I am so glad that horror fans born today will get to see more female directors, more female-led franchises, and more badass final girls. In much the same way as I wish I'd seen more queer horror that appealed to me, I wish I had seen more feminist horror that appealed to me when I was younger.

What I had growing up was Argento.

My parents considered his work—*Suspiria* in particular—to be cinema. Art. If I was interested in watching old Italian movies, I was only ever going to be encouraged in that endeavor. It was nice to see this work that was about women, and what women were capable of (even if those things are not always positive). These themes are touched on in nearly all of Argento's work, and are no doubt made stronger in this film by the writing contributions of Argento's first wife, Daria Nicolodi. As her daughter states in the documentary *Dario Argento Panico*, "I recognize a lot of my mother in this story."[4] I think this is probably one of the earliest experiences that I had of finding a horror film that, even in such beautiful abstraction, gave me a stronger sense of identity.

It can be hard to quantify the way you resonate with a particular work of art. For a long time I struggled to put my feelings about this movie into words, to the extent that I might well have left it out of the book entirely were it not for one thing: my feelings were vindicated.

In 2018, Luca Guadagnino gave us what is arguably one of the finest horror remakes ever put to screen. I may have buried the lede in this chapter because while no one has ever recommended Argento's *Suspiria* to me as a queer film, I'm not sure I have ever met a lesbian who has not recommended Guadagnino's *Suspiria*.

The movie also follows Suzy Bannion, who enrolls at a dance academy run by active practitioners of the occult. The experience, while also heavily stylized and surreal, follows a more linear structure that feels more willing to explore the experiences of its cast.

---

4. In the documentary, Asia Argento also describes *Suspiria* as the "beginning of the end" of her parents' relationship. She believes her mother wrote the main role for herself despite not ultimately being cast in the film. "It was a resentment until the end of her days."

Guadagnino's interpretation sees the underlying energy of the film solidified into queer themes that are then expanded on. There is a stronger focus on the real-world politics of the 1970s backdrop; however, I was more personally moved by the sense of otherness within the dance company and the importance of self-expression within a rigid structure. The script, visuals, and themes are all more definably queer in this modern adaptation.

And yet.

What makes it such a masterful remake is that it's not just a modernization. It's not retelling the exact same stories with the same characters. It doesn't feel as though it's overstepping any bounds by making sweeping changes because it feels as though it is in conversation with the original.

While I do highly recommend the 2018 *Suspiria* as a well-loved, and more obviously Prideful film, I wholeheartedly recommend that you start at the beginning with the 1977 version that breathed it into life. The immaculate visuals, the colorful lighting, and the powerful soundtrack all culminate to create a viewing experience that is unforgettable.

HAUSU
(1977) 
THEY
CALLED
HER
GORGEOUS

"I'm not sure Obayashi necessarily knew what was scary, but he certainly knew what was freaky."

—Nicholas Rucka, *Horror's Greatest*

Vital Statistics

Directed by Nobuhiko Obayashi
Written by Chiho Kastura
Cinematography by Yoshitaka Sakamoto
Edited by Nobuo Ogawa
Starring Kimiko Ikegami as Gorgeous, Miki Jinbo as Kung Fu,
and Yōko Minamida as Auntie
1977, Japan, 88 min.

977 was a great year for foreign horror films that would come to be wholeheartedly embraced by certain facets of the queer community. In the same year that Argento gave us *Suspiria*, Japanese director Nobuhiko Obayashi gave us his surreal horror comedy *Hausu*, known in America as *House*.

The early 2000s saw a surge of J-horror popularity in the States thanks to American remakes of 90s Japanese horror films such as *Ringu* and *Ju-on*, known here as *The Ring* and *The Grudge*, respectively. These films deal with isolated settings and family trauma, which *Audition* director Takashi Miike hypothesizes is in no small part influenced by the popularity of *The Texas Chain Saw Massacre* in Japan. They also paved the way for Americans to get their hands on *House*, which also deals with family trauma in a location isolated from the city, just in a more colorful way.

The film's cheery soundtrack, over-the-top stylings, and satirical approach to its characters made it instantly unforgettable. It also lent an air of flamboyance that made it ripe for interpretation of its themes.

The movie follows high schooler Gorgeous and her six friends who are spending their vacation in the countryside with Gorgeous's ailing Aunt. The girls, who like Gorgeous are all nicknamed and subsequently presented by one characteristic apiece, get picked off one by one over the course of the trip. Ultimately it is revealed that the Aunt who has been hosting them is actually a witch who should have died many years ago, and is sustaining herself by feeding off the lifeforce of unwed girls who wander into the house.

There is no one singular reason why *Hausu* struck a chord for those in the community who have watched it, but rather several aspects of the story and presentation that contribute to the overall feeling of being seen.

The first thing that resonated with me about *Hausu* as a potentially queer narrative is the story of transcendence. The Aunt's powers as a witch slowly transform her throughout the course of the movie until she and Gorgeous become one entity. Not only is this a surprisingly bleak transformation arc about the loss of identity, but it serves as a tale of generational trauma, unrequited love, and the impact of isolation.

Second is the recurring component of obsession. Gorgeous is obsessed with being centered in much the same way that her Aunt is obsessed with her fiancé who died in the Second World War—something that is framed almost as a personal attack rather than a needless tragedy. This is reflected, and to a certain degree reinforced, by the simplicity of the characters' identities all being boiled down to a single characteristic. They all have one label, one thing that is important enough to them to define their entire lives and relationships to one another.

Finally, the third and most striking aspect that spoke to me was the overall flamboyant nature of the entire movie. The pining and transcendence and constant need to reaffirm labels might give the story queer undertones, but that's the only subtle part of the film. The music, colors, special effects, characterizations, set designs, transitions, and dialogue are all so over the top as to make the viewing experience unforgettable. Even the death scenes carry a larger than life sort of whimsy that can leave you smiling through the unease.

Memorable. Fun. Iconic.

It speaks not only to the experience of watching, but to the cleverness at a merchandizing level. Despite the movie's lack of presence in popular horror spaces, it is not at all uncommon for me to see *Hausu* shirts or dresses or even swimsuits pop up at horror or even Pride events. There's something so alluringly silly and vibrant about the movie that it really does seem to capture the hearts of people who are also, dare I say, silly and vibrant.

I would also like to touch on the relationship between Gorgeous and her group of friends. Normally I find it reductive to look for sapphic or queer subtext in stories about female friendships. We have so few instances where women or girls are depicted in supportive roles for one another. Media—and I'd argue horror media in particular—often wants to turn those relationships into something that feels more forced or fetishized.

Something that I find particularly comforting about *Hausu* is how reminiscent of real life I found the female friendships that it depicts. This ties in to another queer wishlist item of found family, which felt further reinforced by the group's insistence on constant labels as opposed to proper names. This aspect of the movie, which is clearly an exaggeration of how poorly horror films handled characterizations in that era, came full circle into feeling authentic again because it is done so lovingly.

I know that when I feel comfortable in a circle with my friends, I don't mind leaning into or playing up aspects of my identity that happen to align with pansexual stereotypes. This doesn't feel so terribly different than Melody being nicknamed after her only hobby or Mac making little quips about her appetite.

This is such a singular film, and its unlikely balancing of grounded relationships and absolutely impossible kills just works. It's unsettling. It's funny. Despite all odds, it's actually pretty cozy, and it's been gratifying to see it strike a chord with so many others of my community. While many of my upcoming recommendations are conditional, based on your tastes, sensitivities, and potential triggers, *Hausu* is one that I wholeheartedly recommend everyone watch at least once just for the experience.

POSSESSION
(1981)
WHAT
THE FUCK
DID I JUST
WATCH?

“. . . a film about a woman who fucks an octopus.”

—Andrzej Żuławski (allegedly)

Vital Statistics

Directed by Andrzej Żuławski
Written by Andrzej Żuławski
Cinematography by Bruno Nuytten
Edited by Mari-Sofi Dubus and Suzanne Lang-Willar
Starring Isabelle Adjani as Anna/Helen, Sam Neill as Mark,
and Heinz Bennent as Heinrich
1981, France/Germany, 124 min.

verybody needs to strap in for this one. *Possession* is a movie
that's almost as difficult to talk about as it is to watch. The
deeper you get into the film, the less hold reality seems to
have on the plot, which is open to so much interpretation that
it's almost impossible to summarize. The history of the film
and its influences are also so numerous and troubled that even
surface-level context can be tricky.

Before we get too deep into it, I want to pull back the curtain
on this project just a touch. My rough draft of this book saw an
average of about three or four handwritten pages per movie,
with annotations about things I wanted to research further. Most
of the movies got an additional page or two of condensed notes
that I chopped up and blended back into my initial thoughts
about the film and how it had affected me. I took eight pages of
notes for *Possession* after I'd already written my initial essay. Eight.
That is over double the amount of space that I devoted to any
other recommendation on this list, and I honestly feel like I may
understand less about the movie than I did when I picked it.

Every question that I had about an artistic choice sent me
down a rabbit hole. I was tracking down Polish science fiction. I
was studying the Berlin Wall. I was Googling marriage counsel-
ing techniques and custody laws internationally in the 70s. This
one nearly broke me, and so much of what I learned is totally off
topic and unusable for this project.

I bring this all up to say that *Possession* is complicated. It was a
product of its time and climate and the tenuous mental state of

its director Andrzej Żuławski, who was inspired to write this after his own divorce. *Queer Tastes* very nearly became a book about this one title, and please understand that I'm doing my best to make it digestible in a single chapter.

The story follows Mark, who has returned home to his wife Anna, despite pressure from his government to resume his work as an international spy. She wants to end their relationship because she has fallen out of love with him. Though she denies it initially, there is also another man in the picture, Heinreich, who feels that his spiritual prowess and sexual compatibility give him a claim to Anna.

Mark becomes obsessive and abusive, denying Anna access to their son Bob unless she agrees to stay with him. They get increasingly violent with one another. He gets in contact with Heinreich and hires a private investigator to try to control his wife while also starting up an affair with Bob's teacher, who looks almost exactly like Anna.

Anna, in the meantime, is living in an apartment with a creature that seems to be growing from the walls. She feeds it the people who come snooping around, and it takes on more of their features between its tentacles. Not only does she confess to sleeping with it, but this is later depicted graphically onscreen when we get the full reveal of the creature in its final evolution.

Anna and Mark die in a shoot-out with police on the stairs of her apartment building, but Anna and her monstrous lover have already completed their second doppelgänger of Mark, which successfully escapes the scene. The movie ends with Bob, left at home with the Anna doppelgänger, hiding in the tub (and potentially drowning) to the sound of what seems to be bomber planes flying overhead.

The experience of watching *Possession* for the first time is one that it's hard to forget, and it's really no wonder why critics have had such a field day trying to make sense of this thing. The movie was relatively well received upon its release, earning its lead Isabelle Adjani three Best Actress Awards including the César, the French equivalent of the Oscars. That seemed to soften the regret that Adjani expressed about taking the role, though both she and Sam Neill described themselves as "psychically scarred for life" after their performances as Anna and Mark.

I have no doubt that as time goes on, we will see more praise for the movie in queer circles. I think the only reason it's not a larger part of the LGBTQIA+ conversation already is because American audiences didn't get to see Żuławski's original version until 2021. There was an instant surge in popularity for the title in the States, but it's the sort of layered film that demands some distance to ponder everything you've seen.

Żuławski was a complicated figure.

Some of the strongest themes—not just in *Possession*, but in his entire body of work—could be viewed favorably or not by progressive audiences. He had a very jaded relationship to politics, as growing up in Poland had left his family oppressed first by fascism and then by communism. His first film, inspired by a book his mother wrote, was about a man who joins the resistance against the Nazis during World War II. His second film got him banned from working in his own country, and he had to move to France to continue his craft. (This explains much of the French influence that creeps into *Possession*.) His political affiliations could perhaps best be described as angry, but I think the affinity for resisting the government throughout his work is something that is felt strongly by the counterculture, even today.

Possession also reveals interesting insight into Żuławski's view of women. Anna is depicted as something frightening and monstrous, but the lens through which the audience views this is quite telling. The horror doesn't come from Anna's needs or her acting on them; it comes from Mark's failure to understand her. The idea that he can be so disgusted and so in love and so broken up over her is what grounds their otherwise nonsensical dialogue throughout the film.

Although it is not a particularly flattering portrayal of women, or marriage for that matter, I think the complexity and nuance make it one of the most powerful. There is an undeniable sense of empathy for Anna, even when we see her at her worst.

The timeline of *Possession* and its place in the LGBTQIA+ community is honestly frustrating. While it was incredibly bold and experimental in its time, it was plagued with distribution issues, including initially being banned in the UK. The first international cut of the film was edited down into an incomprehensible creature feature that was missing about a third of the original's runtime, and featured many scenes out of order. While it's rapidly gaining cult status, there wasn't a chance to appreciate it in the years it could have had the biggest impact on transgressive horror.

In so many early queer films, LGBTQIA+ audiences identified with the monsters. Looking back at classics like *Frankenstein*, it was not just the sense of otherness that made us feel for the monster—it was society's violent reaction to anything they couldn't comprehend. Media over the decades taught us that being different and showing off such differences would turn the world against us. *Possession*, in all of its chaos, strikes at the other side of the coin: the unknown terror of being both vulnerable and seen.

DEADLY GAMES
(1982)

A
WOMAN'S
UNDERSTANDING
OF GAY MEN

"Do you always kiss strange people?"
—Keegan, *Deadly Games*

Vital Statistics

Directed by Scott Mansfield
Written by Scott Mansfield
Cinematography by R. Michael Stringer
Edited by Stuart Eisenberg
Starring Jo Ann Harris as Keegan Lawrence, Sam Groom as
Roger Lane, and Steve Railsback as Billy Owens
1982, USA, 95 min.

For the majority of this book, I have tried to find movies that are representative of my own experience in some way. There are titles that have given me deeper insight into my preferences, my gender, and my ties to the community as a whole. *Deadly Games* is different in that regard, as it's the one movie I chose for an aspect of queer culture that I don't have any experience with: being a gay man.

My insight into that side of the community comes entirely from outsider observations, years of watching horror movies, and practice identifying tropes. It's an area I don't feel as qualified to discuss, but I wanted to at least address it as a blind spot. After all, this is a topic that does inform my tastes, the recommendations I've chosen, and the way I approach them—even if it only affects them by its general absence from the text.

There are actually a lot of movies that I'd like to talk about in this chapter while discussing media trends, but hopefully it will be apparent by the end why *Deadly Games* in particular won out.

The movie follows reporter Keegan Lawrence, who has returned to her hometown following the news of her sister's death. She ends up involved with the cop in charge of the investigation, Roger Lane. He is not only married, but wrapped up in a sort of codependent friendship with the owner of the local movie theater, Billy Owens. The three of them all get closer, even as more murders occur in the town.

Keegan eventually shoots the masked killer, revealing afterward that it was Roger. Billy sees that she's shot his friend, and the movie actually ends mid-shot as he's swooping down to kill her and get his revenge.

One of my favorite aspects of the film is the death scenes. They have a sort of classic whodunit style shot from the killer's POV and the details of the murders all correlate to squares of a monster-themed board game that Roger and Billy play together in the theater basement where Roger eventually dies.

I'm a big sucker for board games, tales of the media-obsessed, and theater settings, so just on a personal level this is the rare 80s slasher that I think doesn't get enough attention.

It was also fairly filled with progressive, if not actively queer subtext. The relationships in the movie are described as modern and open, which I found progressive for the era if not exactly flawless representation. (Roger is fairly abusive to the wife he's in an "open" relationship with, not to mention a serial killer, so obviously not ideal.)

There's a scene where Roger takes Keegan on a date to the movie theater for a private screening that is just the two of them and Billy. The night ends with them drinking and playing games in the basement, and it's shot in a way where it seems as though all three of them are on a date. This fills my little polyamorous heart with so much joy. In that instant, I genuinely did see a little piece of my sort of queerness reflected in *Deadly Games*.

There's also a recurring theme from my first pick, *Rebecca*, where I spoke about obsession being a type of intimacy in the land of queer subtext. Billy's unflinching willingness to kill the one woman who likes him in order to avenge Roger certainly plays into that, and thus felt fitting thematically on my list.

Were it more popular today, *Deadly Games* would undoubtedly have an aggressive queer fanbase writing articles about the doomed relationship of Roger and Billy. I don't have to imagine too much, because the 1990s saw another pair of media-obsessed young men willing to kill for one another whose movie did rise to instant icon status on release.

I'm talking of course about Wes Craven's 1996 film, *Scream*.

One thing that I have noticed in my years online is that the shipping[5] of characters is treated very differently depending on whether the characters in question are men or women. There's this sort of abstract, sapphic longing that is still present today in ships between women, and it's in stark contrast to the very overt sort of fan edits that I see when both characters are men. These pairings can get so intense that they can retroactively change the subtext of the source material, or impact the canon of future works attached to the IP. The funniest example that comes to mind is how fans were so loud about the way that Dr. Lawrence Gordon clings to Adam in the bathroom of the first *Saw* movie that their characters end up in love in the unlicensed *Saw* musical. (Know that there's a version of this project where this chapter is just me defending my opinion that the unlicensed *Saw* musical is closer to the canon than the actual ninth installation of the *Saw* franchise—but I decided to spare you.)

It's a fun story, but that musical is still a fan project so of course fan theories would be accepted. To turn my attention back to *Scream*, fan reactions seem to have had an actual effect on how the first movie is viewed. So many people saw Stu and Billy as a couple that it's become increasingly less likely that someone just now being introduced to *Scream* would read them as friends rather than partners.

After I'd already started work on this project (and after I thought I had my final movies selected—ha!), Matthew Lillard (who played Stu Macher) made a bold statement at Massachusetts's Silver Scream convention where he referred to himself and Skeet Ulrich as "the first husbands of horror." When I tracked down the quote from PinkNews for clarification, the extra context didn't exactly help. "I love standing up and saying we are the first gay couple ever in a horror movie and

---

5. Shipping, for those readers who are not chronically online, is a term for fans expressing their desire for two people, often fictional characters, to end up together.

there's nothing they can fucking say about it. You can't touch it, you can't take it away."

In context of the full quote, I will say that the message was fairly positive. I don't mind at all that Lillard is confirming his mindset in a role or his intention for how he played Stu, and I do genuinely love the attitude of cursing at homophobes. I'm not even going to be a downer and point out that there's a difference between an actor's interpretation of a script and how the lines are written (in part because I don't think screenwriter Kevin Williamson, a gay man, would argue with this interpretation). But I do take issue with the idea that they were the first gay couple ever in a horror movie, because no, of course they weren't.

If we are adding Billy and Stu to the canon of queer horror characters, then I think it's only fair to add the other gay characters who are queer coded with at least the same level of intimacy. The relationship between them is not any more romantic than the relationship between Billy and Roger in *Deadly Games*—and I only bring this movie up because I liked it. It predates *Scream* by fourteen years, but it's also not the first depiction of a gay couple ever in a horror movie.

Gay men seem to have had a very similar trajectory in their representation to gay women, with many queer-coded adaptations in the silent era, ramping up to a sort of golden era just before the Hays Code was instituted in 1930, and then more actively enforced starting in 1934. Even after that, subtext and plausible deniability allowed directors to get away with a lot. Alfred Hitchcock was making movies about gay men, with *Rope* (a movie about two men committing murder together) being one of the most frequently cited examples. Even in my own analysis of *Rebecca*, I drew comparison to Dracula and Renfield because it is one of the most famous examples of an on-screen horror relationship between two men.

I've gotten very far away from the delightful promiscuity of *Deadly Games*, and into territory where I acknowledge I am far from an expert. I would not wish to speak with too much authority on the representation of gay men as that is a group I myself am not a part of. However, in the broader context of being queer and seeking representation in horror, I feel comfortable saying that we should not be erasing the characters that paved the way for us to be seen. We don't call Big John and Little John from *Halloween Kills* the first husbands of horror just because they were more openly a couple than Billy and Stu, who likewise shouldn't be held up as the first on the scene.

THE TOXIC AVENGER (1984)

COMMUNITY, COUNTERCULTURE, AND POLITICAL INCORRECTNESS

"Still one of the most offensive
movies ever made, even by
exploitation standards."

—Joe Bob Briggs

Vital Statistics

Directed by Michael Herz and Lloyd Kaufman
Written by Joe Ritter
Cinematography by James London and Lloyd Kaufman
Edited by Richard W. Haines
Starring Mitch Cohen as the Toxic Avenger, Andree Maranda
as Sara, and Pat Ryan Jr. as Mayor Peter Belgoody
1984, USA, 82 min.

I n my *Suspiria* chapter I spoke about how art films gave me some early overlap with queer communities I otherwise didn't feel I had much in common with. I was delighted to find out the same was true on the other side of the taste spectrum in the form of midnight movies.

Midnight movies emerged as their own tradition in the 1950s, named after the time slot in which they were usually aired on TV. A lot of cheap, schlocky, low-budget horror films aired after it was assumed all the sensible people had gone to bed, and often they were presented by a flamboyant host. Los Angeles had Vampira, Philadelphia had Zacherly, Cleveland had Ghoulardi, and these larger than life personalities served to make the experience even better. Being a millennial, stuck in between the worlds of cable and streaming, my love for midnight movies started with midnight screenings, where old movies would be played for cheap at participating arthouse theaters.

This was something that wasn't originally represented in my recommendations list, because so many of the midnight movies that came to mind were already staples of queer culture. Most of them are creature features, a subgenre I feel is entirely encompassed by LGBTQIA+ culture without my help. The biggest and most successful midnight movie—both in after-hours television programming and in event-style theatrical screenings—is of course *The Rocky Horror Picture Show.*

Not only does *Rocky Horror* get talked to death, but I personally have a complicated relationship to it. Along with many vampire or werewolf films, it was a huge source of me not feeling queer enough to enjoy queer spaces when I was still struggling with labels. Its importance in the history of the community has made it a monolith above all critique in some circles.

The music never scratched the itch in my musical theater brain, and I never found it particularly scary—meaning it didn't scratch the horror itch in my brain either. As an edgy teen who had heard "Time Warp" at every Halloween party since forever, it was a lot easier to just dig my heels in, say I didn't like it, and let every gay person I knew tell me it was because I was straight.

Though I retroactively can appreciate the film's influence, and the bravery of Tim Curry's performance as Dr. Frank-N-Furter, I am just as happy not to use one of my recommendations on the most famous queer movie of all time in my list about underappreciated queer films.

But I decided in revisions that midnight movies were still important. I was watching Elvira present movies before I came out of the closet, and before Cassandra Peterson was even out publicly. As a lazy, movie-loving introvert, the most regular event I share with any of my queer friends is staying up on Fridays to livestream *The Last Drive-In* with Joe Bob Briggs. This sense of community I feel with his Mutant Family is so much like what I used to feel watching midnight movie screenings, and what I sometimes felt I was missing from queer movie nights locally. He and his guests have been quoted often in my research for this project because not only does he cater to even the queerest of tastes, but he's also been such a source of inspiration for me to engage further with the movies I watch and the people watching with me.

In that spirit, I chose a movie that actually celebrated its fortieth anniversary on *The Last Drive-In*, and that brings the best and the worst gay representation along for the ride: *The Toxic Avenger*.

It's one of the most famous and beloved films distributed by Troma Entertainment. The company was founded by Lloyd Kaufman and Michael Herz in 1974 to "disrupt media" and has become one of the most successful independent production companies. They've created several original franchises, distributed hundreds of other titles, and kept full creative control for over fifty years already. They are a testament to what indie filmmakers can accomplish, though they also have a reputation of making films that are vulgar and tasteless. Their unflinching approach to storytelling and overall lack of censorship has given Troma films some of the most diverse representation, and also some of the most problematic. This is true for most of their catalogue, but is particularly easy to spot in *The Toxic Avenger*.

The movie follows Melvin Ferd, a janitor at the Tromaville health club where all the shadiest people seem to congregate. He gets on the wrong side of a gang, and in a revenge prank gone wrong, he is pushed into toxic waste that transforms him into a sort of antihero known as The Toxic Avenger. He stops crimes around the city, falls in love, and earns enough goodwill in the community that the military chooses to spare him even against orders from their corrupt mayor.

The movie features not only a gay slur (which it uses frequently) but just about every other slur there is. It broke all the rules that movies had to follow to maintain decency at the time. The dog died. The kid died. There were closeups of the dead dog and kid. The language was so obscenely offensive that audiences today are just as shocked (if not more so) than they were in the 80s when the film failed to get a wide release in theaters. (This failure is not surprising: almost a third of the audience is reported to have walked out of the premiere during the first onscreen hit and run.)

There are multiple gay characters who are villains in *The Toxic Avenger*. I'm not even going to try to defend this pick by pointing out the recurring couple of gay, fitness-obsessed hairdressers who stand up for Toxie at the end of the film after fighting about which one of them could get him into bed.

What I will say is that I just don't have it in my heart to be put off by such an equal-opportunity offender with such a wholesome message overall. The charm of Troma films was that they were made in poor taste. It was part of the gross-out humor, it was part of the cutting satire, and it's one of the reasons why so many of them have held their unique spot in the horror space. As the movie's creator Lloyd Kaufman said during the fortieth anniversary special, "the joy of being deep underground is that you can do anything you want. It's liberating."

It's also refreshing.

The Toxic Avenger is the sort of movie that couldn't be made today. Case in point, when it got a $60 million remake in 2023 with a star-studded cast, it was cleaned up considerably. I loved the final product (and its novelization by Adam Cesare) but the project, by necessity, lacked a lot of the humor that made the original so shocking and provocative. The anti-establishment theme of the original was strengthened, but the imperfect representation was removed—and this goes for the wisecracking gay supporting cast as well as for the problematic cross-dressing minions. Even with these modifications, the movie didn't hit theaters until 2025.

I fear inclusivity in media has come at the price of expression. There is so much infighting, even in queer spaces, that the pressure to be perfect can be silencing. The fear of misspeaking is so prevalent, and even well-intentioned parties can be ostracized for making mistakes. The focus, especially online, often feels geared more toward call-outs than real community building.

It's why I think *The Toxic Avenger* works as a community film on so many levels. The community rallies behind Toxie for saving them in the film, and by embracing their monster, they're able to overthrow the corrupt and oppressive government. The movie itself, which built a cult following over decades, one theater or VHS tape at a time, is a quintessential midnight movie that's still bringing the horror community together. The remake carried on the legacy of community-building by partnering with the nonprofit Undue Medical Debt and spending their $5 million marketing budget on relieving medical debt—a central theme in their vision of the story.

I know that modern audiences probably don't have the patience for the original film, but I think anyone like myself who is harder to offend will absolutely fall in love with this classic.

THE SILENCE OF THE LAMBS (1991)

TERMINOLOGY, EXPOSURE, AND GATEWAY MEDIA

"The significance of the moth is change."

—Dr. Hannibal Lecter,
The Silence of the Lambs

Vital Statistics

Directed by Jonathan Demme
Written by Ted Tally
Cinematography by Tak Fujimoto
Edited by Craig McKay
Starring Jodie Foster as Clarice Starling, Anthony Hopkins as
Dr. Hannibal Lecter, Scott Glenn as Jack Crawford, and Ted
Levine as Jame "Buffalo Bill" Gumb
1991, USA, 118 min.

believe that more representation is inherently good representation. My recommendations thus far have spanned five decades of horror, and none of it has been in a vacuum. The good, openly queer characters followed the questionable openly queer characters, who followed the subtextually queer characters who followed the subtextually queer villains. It has not been exactly that linear, but it has been a pattern of beginning conversations, fighting for space, and improving over time.

There is one thing that I genuinely like about myself, and it's my relationship to representation in media. Movies, books, games—these are all just forms of storytelling for me. Like any kind of fiction, they can serve as an excellent gateway into experiences that are far different than my own.

The keyword there is gateway.

No one depiction of an experience should be the final stop in your journey to learn about communities different from your own. Even in an ideal world where marginalized communities had the same platforms as straight, white, cisgender men, not every single depiction would be perfect. No one person can tell a story that fully encompasses the experience of everyone in their demographic, nor would I want them to. That would strip away the variety, the personality, and I think the power from a lot of the art we are still conversing about years after its release.

The Silence of the Lambs was my introduction into the concept of transness. As a cisgender woman, it certainly isn't up to me to decide if the inclusion of trans themes was a net positive or not.

I know many argue that *The Silence of the Lambs* was, and continues to be, harmful to the way transgender ideology is depicted onscreen. In a blog post about calling out transphobia in the media, Savannah Staubs said: "In addition to demonizing and stigmatizing gender fluidity, *Silence of the Lambs* idealizes normative gender expression."[6]

I want to take a look at the movie, the backlash, and the decades of conversations that have followed in its wake.

The film follows FBI agent-in-training Clarice Starling, who is given the opportunity to interview a psychiatric patient, Dr. Hannibal Lecter. She uses his insights and connections to get information about an ongoing investigation into Buffalo Bill, a serial killer who takes skin from the women he murders. Later it's revealed that he's wearing the skin he harvests.

There is one scene that has been a particular source of controversy since the film's release. Dr. Lecter suggests that Buffalo Bill places moths into the mouths of his victims because they are symbolic of change, and he too wishes to change. Clarice, picking up the implication, pushes against it. "There's no correlation in literature between transsexualism and violence. Transexuals are very passive." Later on in their conversation, Dr. Lecter delivers a line that would come to haunt the film's legacy. "Billy is not a real transsexual, but he thinks he is. He tries to be."

There's a lot to unpack already.

First, the term "transsexual" has fallen by the wayside in favor of the term "transgender." From an etymological standpoint, "transsexual" is a label under the term "transgender" but it has become less socially acceptable because of its historical ties to transmedicalism—the sentiment that a trans person can only be recognized as their preferred gender after physically altering their body with surgery or hormones. Not all trans people are interested in altering their bodies or "proving" their transness.

6. "The Not So Hidden Transphobia in Silence of the Lambs," 2014, thesociologicalcinema.com/blog/the-not-so-hidden-transphobia-in-silence-of-the-lambs

The shift to "transgender" as the more inclusive and socially accepted term reflects the freedom of gender expression and an individual's right to qualify their own gender.

As a small aside, this was something that I struggled to learn because the first trans woman I was close to grew up with the term transsexual, had medically transitioned, and chose to continue using the term because she felt it was the best label for her. I'm not in the business of policing anyone's preferred language for themselves, but it was a hard habit to break as I moved into other circles that took offense to the term.

Secondly, and perhaps this is evident from my first point, the framework through which the average American understands the trans experience is far more nuanced in 2025 than it was in 1991 (or especially 1989 when the story is estimated to take place). We've stepped away from the idea of men wanting to surgically become women, and into the idea of individuals who identify as a gender that doesn't align traditionally with the sex characteristics assigned to them at birth.

When people look back at this scene today, there are a lot of reasons to get offended. There's the outdated terminology, the harmful framing that someone has to "try" to be trans, and the filmmakers' belief that a couple throwaway lines about Billy not being associated with the "passive" community in question could shield the production from backlash. None of this even touches on the film's more lasting legacy of transmisogyny—and it is sort of the quintessential fear that transphobes have about trans women.

Whenever someone speaks out against trans rights, they seem to paint this picture of a violent man trying to further oppress women by infiltrating their spaces in some sort of ghoulish woman-suit. The movie can say Billy's not a part of that community, but it's hard to deny that they put a face on that exact fear. This should go without saying, but the fear is completely unfounded. There just aren't reports of men pretending to be women to infiltrate women's spaces that are already so loosely protected—and trans women are particularly vulnerable to such assaults because of discrimination.

I have to point out that the backlash against this movie is nothing new. I don't believe in holding past media accountable to modern sensibilities, and if I did, I likely wouldn't have even brought up this film. But the LGBTQ+ community at the time actually had some pretty harsh critiques of this scene, Ted Levine's depiction of Buffalo Bill, and the movie's handling of the character in general.

There was a prevalent fear that the movie would lead to an uptick in hate crimes against the gay and trans communities, and even in retrospect many people claim this as a negative impact of the film. There are so many factors surrounding this sort of hate and these types of incidents that I don't want to say it's impossible that *The Silence of the Lambs* may have fanned the flames, but largely the numbers don't suggest that it did. The data on these types of hate crimes has only been collected and reported on by the American government since 1990, meaning there would almost have to be an increase in recorded incidents in 1991 because it was the first time that infrastructure existed to make such reports. The one official document that seems to tie the film to hate crimes was a Hate Crimes Violence hearing in 1999 that used the fictional events depicted as a way to help identify real-life hate crimes—which actually supports the idea that having a cultural touchstone to marginalized communities can be beneficial, even if the execution is lacking.

As the discussions of gender politics have gotten more progressive and nuanced, we have a whole array of new ways to say that this film was problematic and flawed. I defer largely to the trans community about how the film and its impact have played into a broader understanding of their struggles.

And yet, here I am recommending it.

As this was my introduction to the idea of the trans experience, I did leave with some wildly inaccurate ideas about what it meant to be trans. My opinion wasn't negative, but it was still a harmful perception of a group that I don't speak for. Had I never learned anything else about the community, I'd have been terribly ignorant. But couldn't the same be said of anything?

I want to bring this chapter back around to the idea of media being a gateway. I learned, incorrectly, about an experience that I had no prior exposure to. Shining a light on it opened up my eyes to learn better from that point. The educational aspect all came after I knew I had a blind spot, and it came in the form of nonfiction pieces written by members of the actual community.

We do not have to rely on fiction to be our only source of information. In fact, we actually should not rely on fiction to be our one source of information, and it's enough sometimes that a movie can introduce you to a new concept.

I consider myself incredibly lucky that there was this cultural touchstone that inspired so many informative pieces. Even if a lot of it is outrage, there's so much material about this movie and its impact and the areas where it failed. I've learned so much by engaging with the countless think pieces that have come out about the film. In much the same way that I think it's helpful to have seen *Psycho* in order to be a part of the discussion, I think it's important to see *The Silence of the Lambs*.

Not for nothing, it's also an incredible film. It won five Academy Awards including Best Picture, the performances are impeccable, the editing is eerie, and it gave us some of the genre's most iconic lines. "I ate his liver with some fava beans and a nice Chianti."

Its rise to popularity also paved the way for the television series *Hannibal* years later, which was widely embraced by the community for the homoerotic tension between Hannibal Lecter and FBI profiler Will Graham.

There is something so human to want to unconditionally defend something we love. There's also something very powerful in admitting that we love something problematic, and allowing ourselves to love it anyway. Acknowledging that things are flawed is an important part of moving society forward.

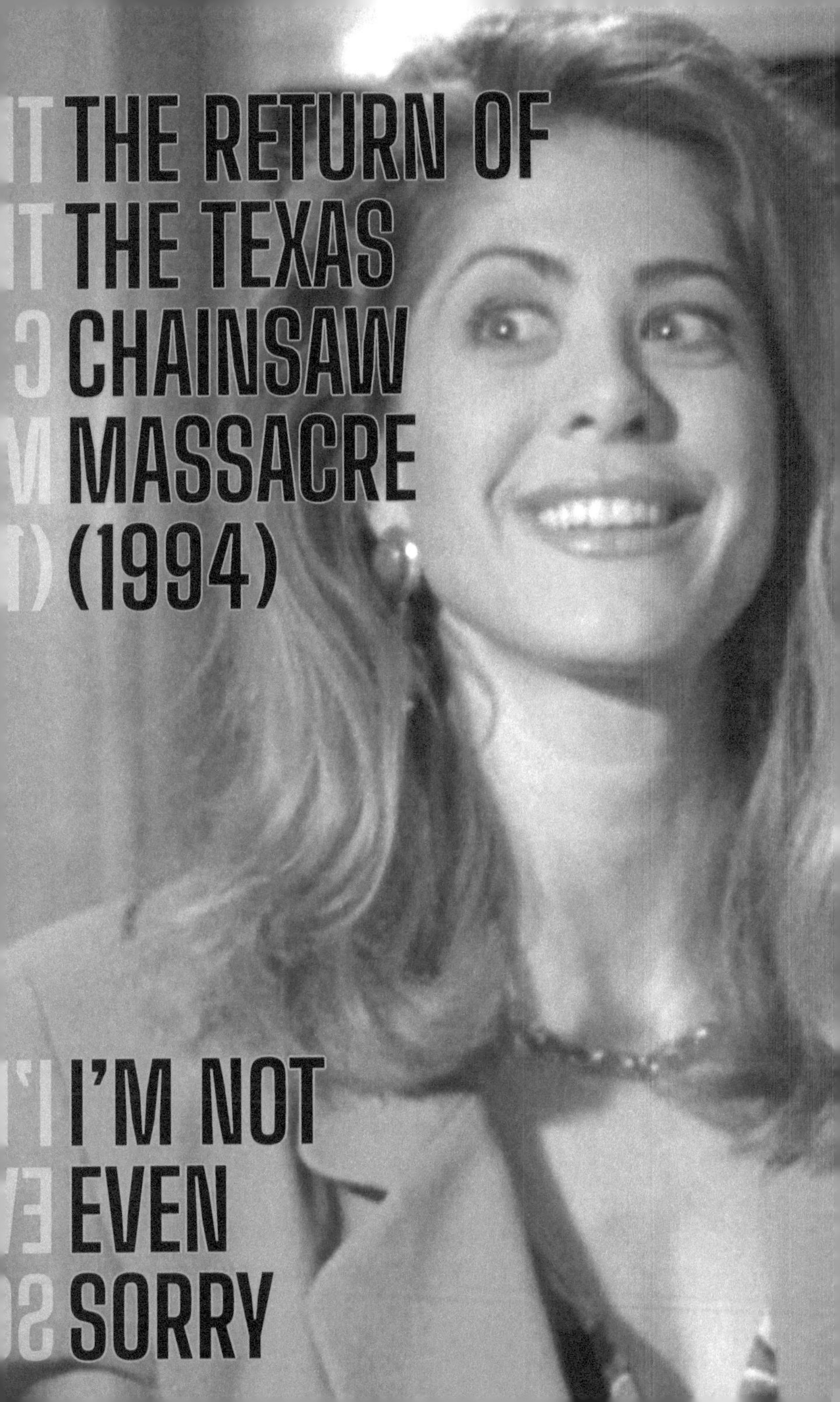

THE RETURN OF THE TEXAS CHAINSAW MASSACRE (1994)

I'M NOT EVEN SORRY

"I'm sure none of it was legal . . . but what an experience."

—Renee Zellweger

Vital Statistics

Directed by Kim Henkel
Written by Kim Henkel
Cinematography by Levie Isaacks
Edited by Sandra Adair
Starring Renée Zellweger as Jenny, Matthew McConaughey as Vilmer, Robert Jacks as Leatherface, and Tonie Perenskey as Darla
1994, USA, 95 min.

While I was working on revisions for this book, I ended up having to trim down my number of recommendations. I cut out the movies I didn't feel as passionately about and combined chapters where I felt I had re-tread territory into a single recommendation. The movie that actually inspired this project didn't make the final cut. But here I am including a second *Texas Chainsaw* movie.

The thought crossed my mind that my feelings about *The Return of the Texas Chainsaw Massacre* could have been a footnote in the chapter where I'm already talking about the franchise. There were so many foundational ideas to cover in that first chapter, though: the movie's exclusion from queer conversations, the important role of aesthetics, the satirization of the gender binary, and the influence it had on some of the other movies I knew were on my list. I didn't want to get distracted and draw focus away from the original film.

But I just couldn't bear to leave out this sequel.

This is a title I feel so passionately about, and it gets so much hate. It doesn't even have a strong cult following and as of the time of editing this book, it boasts only a 16% rating on Rotten Tomatoes with fewer than fifty critic reviews. It's probably my most fun hot take, and absolutely the pinnacle of what I hoped to accomplish with this project. So I hope that you'll indulge me while I talk about my favorite bisexual icon of the 1990s.

In the *Texas Chain Saw Massacre* chapter I talked a little about fans' overall negative reaction to the franchise as a whole. Though the original film is beloved, it's generally regarded as one of the weaker horror franchises overall. Usually people will like two *Texas Chainsaw* films: the original and one sequel that aligns with their particular genre preferences. The black comedy lovers will love the first two. Gorehounds will love the original and the 2003 remake of the same title. Strange, strange people who I don't understand will love the original as well as the 2022 Netflix followup—the only one of the entire series that I actively dislike.

Even before we get into the queerness of it all, I differ from my fellow *Chainsaw* fans because I just can't get enough of this franchise. With the one notable exception, they're either masterpieces or they're so bad they're good, and I love them in either instance. Those are my two favorite types of horror movies, after all.

The Return of the Texas Chainsaw Massacre falls solidly into the "so bad it's good" category despite starring Renée Zellweger and Matthew McConaughey, who would go on to have careers more successful than any of the actors from the original. Kim Henkel, who co-wrote the script for the 1974 film, returned to the franchise as writer and director with the intention of dialing up the ridiculous nature of the family and playing with caricatures.

The story, such as it is, follows four teens whose car breaks down after prom. They try to get assistance but find themselves separated and getting picked off by a deranged, cultlike family in the woods that is led by McConaughey's character, Vilmer.

Everything is so exaggerated in this film. It lacks Hooper's confidence behind the camera, and the stellar editing team, so the overall experience is far less effective than in the original, but it is not without a couple of very striking visuals. I noticed while watching Shudder's 2022 *Queer for Fear* documentary series that a passing mention of Leatherface's crossdressing is supplemented by footage not of the original dinner scene, but of its counterpart in this particular sequel. I thought that was a fun bit of trivia, but Leatherface and his very gaudy mask actually have nothing to do with why I picked this.

I picked it because of Darla.

Vilmer, the cannibalistic cult leader with a mechanical leg, is in a relationship with one of the most unapologetically bisexual characters I've ever seen in horror. Darla might be my favorite character in the franchise—in no small part because she is totally out of place. Vilmer treats her poorly; they fight; she seems disgusted by the family, their manners, and their house. There is a predatory element to Tonie Perenski's portrayal of the character, but she also seems far more interested in Zellweger's Jenny than in actually participating in the murders.

In fact, in what is, hands down, my favorite scene, Darla completely botches her chance to kill one of the teens herself. She encounters them already injured, lying in the road, and in the path of her car. After half-heartedly beating them with a stick, she gets bored, gives into their demands to stop, and finds someone else to take care of the murder for her. It's probably one of the funniest horror moments ever put to film, and I think it's a shame that it's slept on.

Brilliant comedic stylings aside, *The Return of the Texas Chainsaw Massacre* revisits and challenges the idea of a traditional family dynamic and gender roles. In much the same way that The Cook was introduced as a member outside the family in the original, the audience doesn't initially know that Darla has any sort of connection to the killers when she's introduced. There's the hope that she's going to be a savior to the teens before she ultimately lures them into more danger.

Vilmer ignores her, puts her down, gets violent with her, and all of her focus still seems to be on Jenny. This will not be the last time that I pick a movie that uses violence as a metaphor for attraction, but it is one of my favorite examples of bisexual bloodlust—where the sensual nature of a character's killing or torturing reads as a stand-in for sexual desire for both men and women.

So much of Darla's time onscreen is filled with looks of longing, gentle stroking of Jenny's hair, and overly familiar touches. It is nearly impossible, even in the context of a deranged slasher family, to read Darla's body language as anything other than flirtatious.

I think of Darla, in many ways, as a precursor to a more popular character: Baby from Rob Zombie's Firefly trilogy. The character caught a lot of flak for being so overtly sexualized—often at the same time she's being self-infantalized. Many also just found her to be annoying, particularly in the middle installation, *The Devil's Rejects*.

But Baby Firefly is another character whose vaguely defined sexuality was open to interpretation through the violence she commits. She's not as active a participant as either of her brothers, but she does have fun torturing and teasing both the men and women who are trapped in the family's titular *House of 1000 Corpses*. It's perhaps another case of the deranged content and style of the movie keeping marginalized communities somewhat at arm's length.

Darla would have been a safer bet for iconic bisexual rep for women in the 90s–00s as she was intelligent, smartly dressed, and guilty of fewer acts of necrophilia. Her claim to fame was hampered by the fact that this film is so wildly unpopular. Critics didn't care much for it, and issues with the reselling of the home video distribution rights meant that a lot of people didn't even get to see the movie when it was first out, or even first sold. The film was eventually recut and the new version, entitled *The Texas Chainsaw Massacre: The Next Generation*, dipped below the standard 90-minute runtime benchmark for most slashers of the era.

This is another one of those movies that I will recommend to anybody that will listen. I have yet to find another person who likes it, but nothing is going to stop me from trying. I hope that one day the queer community embraces the character of Darla with the same willingness to overlook problematic rep with which it regards Jesse from *A Nightmare on Elm Street 2: Freddy's Revenge*.

PERFECT BLUE) (1997)

OBSESSION, SELF-DOUBT, AND PURITY

"I mean, there's a gap between the image people see of me and what I see myself. *Perfect Blue* is about the tragedy caused by that gap becoming too large."
—Satoshi Kon

Vital Statistics

Directed by Satoshi Kan
Written by Sadayuki Murai
Cinematography by Hisao Shirai
Edited by Harutoshi Ogata
Starring the voices of Junko Iwao as Mima and Rica Matsumoto as Rumi
1997, Japan, 81 min.

efore we can talk about *Perfect Blue* (a movie that I would like
to always be talking about in an ideal world), I feel as though
I should address something. Darren Aronofsky's blatantly
queer masterpiece *Black Swan* will not appear in this book. It
was one of the films that I listed while pitching this project because I thought it would be perfect. It has the polished aesthetic
quality that so many of my peers are attracted to. It has a severe
understanding of femininity that ties into my early sapphic selections. The themes of obsession and identity run through the
plot. The ballet atmosphere could have been a nice nod back to
a Suspirian influence. I love this film, and I'm surprised by how
seldom I see it on queer recommendation lists.

The movie received early criticism for a lesbian sex scene between Mila Kunis and Natalie Portman that I was looking forward
to breaking down and defending in essay form. But although I
do recommend the title, and thought it was worth bringing up, I
instead devote its slot in this project to the movie that inspired it.

Aronofsky has openly admitted how blatantly he takes concepts, themes, and even imagery from Kon's body of work, *Perfect
Blue* in particular. Some of the most striking side-by-side com-
parisons can actually be made between *Perfect Blue* and *Requiem for
a Dream. Black Swan*'s premise of being tormented by an illusory
and more perfect version of yourself, however, is quite reminiscent of the plot synopsis we're about to get into.

Perfect Blue follows Mima, a pop idol in 1990s Japan. She was
one of the singers of the girl group CHAM! before deciding to

pivot into acting. Though she leaves with confidence, she soon finds herself plagued by former fans who hate her for leaving the group to pursue her own interests.

There is a fan blog dedicated to spreading misinformation about Mima, how she is being manipulated by TV producers into acting unlike herself, and eventually how she isn't the "real Mima." Mima begins to confuse her everyday life for the events described in the blog or playing out on her new TV show, and hallucinating an alternate version of herself where she never left CHAM!

The movie was ahead of its time in so many aspects regarding toxic fandom culture, parasocial relationships, and unrealistic expectations for celebrities. The fact that the Mima impersonator is someone close to her (her agent, Rumi) makes the entire thing feel even more like a betrayal.

Rumi's obsession with Mima's "purity" is truly reminiscent of the idol culture in Japan that it's supposed to represent—but I could not help comparing pieces of it to the political climate that celebrities must navigate online today. This is especially true for anyone in the public eye who is openly a part of the LGBTQIA+ community, and must carry the expectations of fans who are desperate to see themselves represented at that level.

Since the invention of social media, long after this film's original release, this sort of toxic behavior has become infinitely more normalized. Celebrities have to deal with the personal opinions of thousands of complete strangers who are trying to hold them to impossible and often contradictory standards. Some of the most appalling examples of this are the people that hold online "funerals" or post "eulogies" for actors and actresses that have come out as trans.

Even as she's finding her footing and gaining more success in the world of acting, Mima finds herself growing less sure about her own identity. She loses time, she hallucinates, she begins to drown in depression and doubt. She looks back at CHAM! and their success without her, and wonders if she wouldn't be happier had she stayed.

This is where *Perfect Blue* has elements of a "road not taken" story, which always makes for a strong queer allegory. I, and many of the people close to me, are fortunate to have strong support systems in our lives. But being a part of the LGBTQIA+ community means leaving behind what your life was before.

Change can be, and often is, an extremely positive experience. It's also one of the most terrifying experiences because it is the shedding of something familiar. In a queer context particularly, it is complete and total reinvention, the loss of a version of yourself. The mental vulnerability that follows is a breeding ground for doubt.

There are what-ifs. There's the panic as you realize it's too late to go back—even sometimes as you're experiencing pressure or incentive to try to return to the way things were, even at the cost of something new you're trying to build. There's nothing worse than showing the world who you truly are and being met with hate for it—especially when that hate is being amplified by the internet.

I'm not sure there is any kind of horror that is more impactful to me than stories of identity that allow themselves to go into truly dark places.

There's a part of *Perfect Blue*, as Mima's sense of self is already crumbling, where she gets pressured by her agent and the TV studios into performing a scene where her character is sexually assaulted. Even in the context of knowing the scene is being staged for a fictional show within the movie, it's so visceral that it's actually harder to watch than a scene later on in the film where someone actually attempts to assault her. Her reaction to that filming is the start of her truly breaking down, dissociating, and buying into this idea that she's become tarnished or dirty.

After filming the scene she is pushed further and further along into a more sexualized identity on the program and its marketing. There's a sunk cost fallacy for her, where she feels she has to keep her new industry happy, having already turned her back on the life where she would have been protected.

It's a terrible comparison to have to make, but for a long time being queer was also considered dirty by the masses. There is an uneasy pressure to please the people in your new life, simply because you know you cannot ever go back to how it was before.

I don't think it was Kon's intention to create any kind of queer allegory with this film, but then again, I don't think it always has to be the intention of the artist to create something that will strike a chord. Sometimes an artist following their own interests and views produces the sort of lasting pieces that will stand the test of time, living on to be interpreted and re-interpreted for generations.

I was lucky enough this last year to catch *Perfect Blue* in a limited theatrical run, and I can honestly say that I don't think I've ever seen an audience so completely wrapped up in what they were watching. Despite the unavoidably dated technology of the late 1990s, the story has proven to be so timeless and transcendent that it resonates with people from all walks of life. If you haven't seen it already, and are in a mental state to handle some of its more graphic elements, I highly recommend checking this one out for its strong themes of identity.

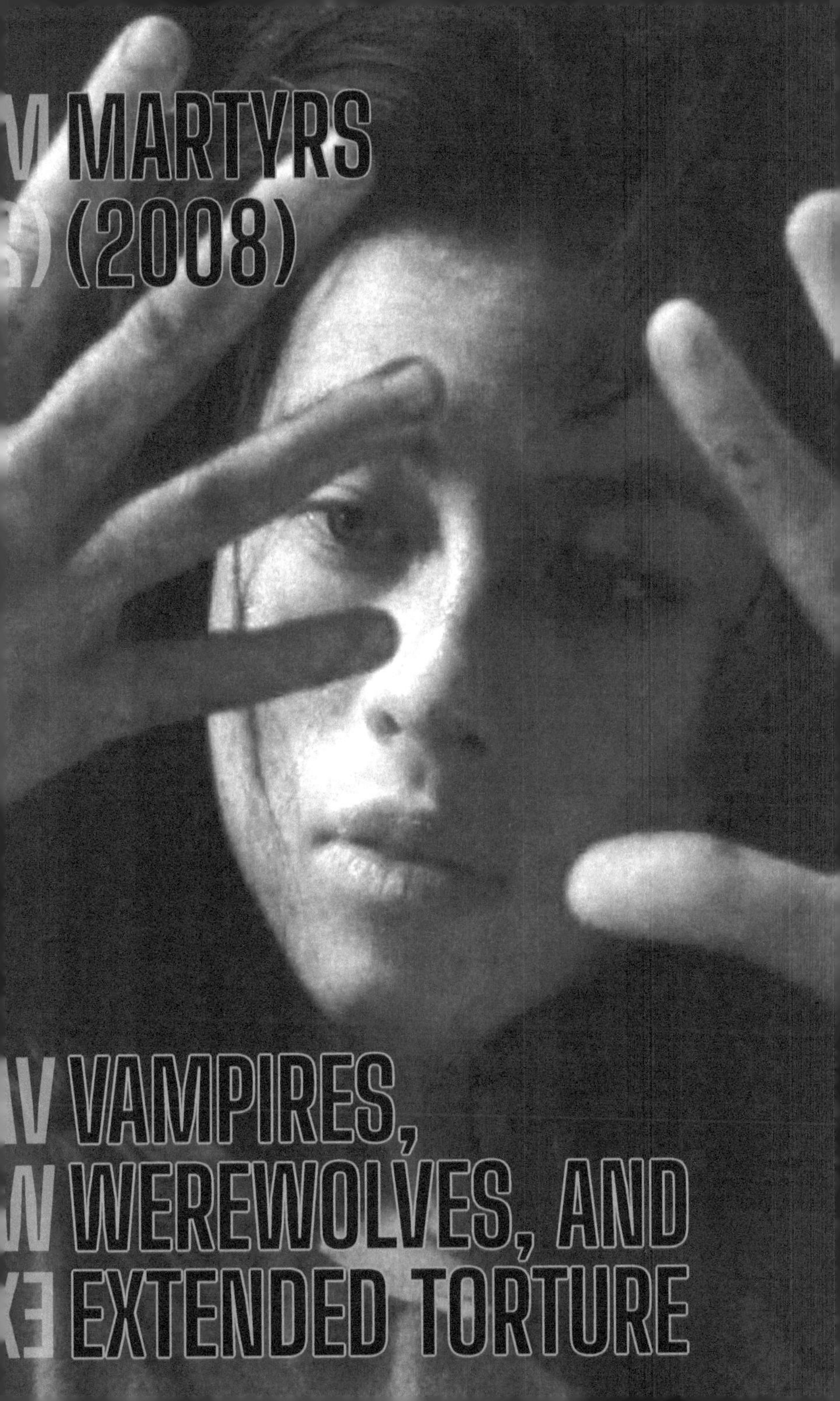

MARTYRS (2008)

"The *Citizen Kane* of torture porn."

—Jamie Flanagan
(who asked me to specify that
they will not watch *Martyrs*)

Vital Statistics

Directed by Pascal Laugier
Written by Pascal Laugier
Cinematography by Stéphane Martin and Nathalie
Moliavko-Visotzky
Edited by Sébastien Prangère
Starring Morjana Alaoui as Lucie, Mylène Jampanoï as Anna,
and Catherine Begin as Mademoiselle
2008, France, 99 min.

When choosing which unconventional and unpopular queer movies I would put in my final list, I was guided by a single, self-imposed rule that I've been building to this entire book: no vampires or werewolves. It's time to let the undead out of their coffins, the lycans off of their chains, and address why I bent over backward to not recommend an entire subgenre of aggressively queer horror.

For the two or three people reading this who have followed my career the last few years, you may already know that I have strong feelings about Pascal Laugier's masterful stroke of the New French Extremity movement, *Martyrs*. It's one of only two films in my adult life that have ever disturbed me. It's one of my top five favorite films of all time. It is, without question, my favorite queer film—and it was actually *Martyrs* that inspired me to come out of the closet. Since then, it's been instrumental to my career as a horror writer—and especially as a horror writer in the queer space.

When I released my debut novella *Revenge Arc*, I had the opportunity to talk about revenge tropes on the *Killer Mediums* podcast, which meant getting to choose two examples of the trope in film. It was the first of many times that I had a platform to properly explain why Laugier's presentation of his narrative informed my own work. Just a year after that I was chosen to have an essay featured in *Divergent Terror: The Crossroads of Queerness and Horror* from Off Limits Press.

My contribution was called "Witness: The Transformative Power of *Martyrs*." It was my first nonfiction work to make it into print, my first time being paid for queer analysis, and it ultimately became the blueprint for *Queer Tastes*. The thesis of the essay was that some members of the LGBTQIA+ community prefer torture porn[7] to werewolf movies, and we also deserve to celebrate our cinematic preferences. "But what if your taste in horror leans more to the extreme?"

I used werewolves as an example because I was drawing from my personal experience in queer spaces and knew more people who preferred werewolves to vampires. (In loving retrospect, I can see that this was as much about my friends being furries as it was about them being queer.) I talked about how important media has always been to me, how passionately I've always felt about the horror genre, and how isolating it can feel to not like the same films that your community likes—all core elements of this project and its introduction.

A lot of the feedback that I got on the essay was kind, but critical. Some felt I had drawn more from anecdotal evidence than the other essayists had. Many people felt personally offended that I didn't like werewolf movies. Mostly, people didn't like how I spoke so lovingly of a film that has been so controversial for its brutality. A small group of readers, however, reached out to me personally after the collection was published to talk to me about how much *Martyrs* meant to them—as a queer person, as a horror fan, or as a woman.

I pitched *Queer Tastes* for all those weirdos who came out of the woodwork because they are my kind of freaks. With that in mind, I wanted to expand on my thoughts from my previous

---

7. The term "torture porn" sprang up in the 2000s as a derogatory way to refer to particularly gruesome horror movies. It has since been embraced and reclaimed by defenders of the subgenre such as myself, who would cite that some of the most terrifying and thought-provoking horror movies of the last twenty years have been written off by the masses as borderline fetish content. This was also a critique of *The Texas Chain Saw Massacre* when it was released, so I have no doubt that time will vindicate my love of the *Saw* franchise ... eventually.

essay and present my new thesis: some queer people prefer torture porn to both werewolves and vampires. There's just no movie I can think of that better expresses why that's the case than my lovely, lovely *Martyrs*.

The film follows Anna, who comes to clean up the crime scene after her friend Lucie murders an entire family over breakfast. Lucie believes that they were responsible for the unspeakable abuse she endured when she was a child. As Anna attempts to clean up the mess, Lucie begins to doubt whether her friend believes her story. We see that she is still plagued by the demons that have followed her since childhood, and that getting her revenge has not bought their silence.

It dances between the genres of psychological and supernatural horror during its opening, tricking you into believing first that it's one thing, and then another entirely. It is only in the final act, after Lucie has committed suicide, that the movie reveals its true nature. Anna learns that her friend's story of being abducted and tortured by this perfectly innocent looking family was true. Their matriarch had imprisoned Lucie for years, and the suffering she had inflicted upon her was truly unimaginable.

The woman was part of a society that subjects women to prolonged periods of suffering with the intention of creating a true martyr. Since she already knew too much from being inside the house, Anna becomes the cult's next victim. Suddenly the unimaginable becomes quite vivid and explicit.

The abuse that Anna goes through onscreen is difficult to watch. She is chained, neglected, force-fed, and beaten to within an inch of her life repeatedly. We see the light slowly and gradually forced out of her in one of the most upsetting montages I've ever witnessed. Only when she fully accepts this as her new reality is she deemed ready for the final stage of her transformation.

This montage lasts a little over eighteen minutes. It feels like an eternity as you're sitting through it. The brutality of the visuals holds nothing back from the viewer—and I can personally assure you that if you're the sort of masochist who revisits this title, it never gets easier to watch.

It's a scene that I find viscerally haunting. It's my least favorite part of every rewatch, despite the impact that it ultimately had on me. It was because this scene lingered, because it scared me, because I was unable to stop thinking about it, that I finally had to ask some difficult questions about myself.

Transformation is the quintessential queer narrative in horror. Yet while I was growing up, I simply didn't see the sort of variety that I wanted in horror transformations. Werewolves have this immense power waiting for them on the other side of what is often depicted as a painful transition, but we know ultimately that they're going to be okay.

Even before werewolves became near-synonomous for queer allegories in horror, we had vampires filling that role. While their transformation is often more ritualistic and seductive, and less primal, it offers a similar premise. There is a bite, there's a transformation, and then there is eternal life filled with taboo pleasures. Vampires may be damned, but they come out the other side with the sort of alluring abilities that could easily sway a mortal into their thrall.

I am unafraid of the pain associated with transformation. My fear comes from the idea of my own mortal weakness—the idea that I might not come out the other side. That was something I wasn't seeing depicted in queer films: the fear of not making it through the transformation at all. Even monsters, who historically have tragic endings, are often killed by humans for what they are rather than for the experience of *becoming* what they are.

It was terrifying to watch *Martyrs* and feel like Anna simply wasn't going to make it through to the other side of her transformation. I'd never seen a movie that made me doubt the survival of a character so much, and that had me so invested in their future. It was scary that I couldn't envision a future for her, and made that much more impactful by the fact I was watching it at a time I was struggling to see a future for myself.

I'd been having doubts for a while that maybe it's not so straight to kiss other women or have several ex-girlfriends online. I was in a straight-passing monogamous relationship at that point in my life, and I kept saying that it didn't matter how straight I was or wasn't because I was straight enough. I was there, and mostly happy, and putting a label on myself could cost the future that I'd been building with a person I cared about.

Watching *Martyrs* and feeling such a genuine fear gave me that deep sort of connection to the movie that I'd seen my friends have to *Ginger Snaps* or to *The Hunger*. It also filled me with a deep-rooted sort of dread that would set the stage for every queer horror movie I'd come to identify with later on; I want movies that are going to upset me and shake up my worldview. Oftentimes they have to go to the darkest places to evoke such things.

Anna does survive, after a fashion. No one could live long in the state that her tormentors leave her in, but she does become the first success story of the organization. Not only does she ascend to true martyrdom, she is the first person to do so who survives long enough to tell them what she's seen on the other side. She relays the information to the organization's leader, Mademoiselle, in the form of a few whispered words that the audience is unable to hear.

"Any story that is about transformation and links transformation with sexuality has to be read as a queer story," Roberto Aguirre said in Shudder's *Queer for Fear* (2022) documentary. The limited series features four episodes. The first centers around gothic horror, and much of the attention is given to *Dracula*. The second episode is largely about classic Universal monsters, and while he is not the focus, much of the attention is again on Dracula. The third episode is about werewolves, and the fourth is about dangerous women (including the sleazy lesbian vampires of the 70s and 80s).

It's a fascinating watch, and I do recommend it, but it's also the sort of documentary that would have convinced me once upon a time that I wasn't really all that queer. The conversations about LGBTQIA+ horror get so focused on these two, very similar subgenres to the exclusion of other examples of transformation themes onscreen.

It was a big decision to exclude all vampire movies and all werewolf movies, especially those with interesting nuances or different takes on the mythology that I think are worthy of exploration. I feel confident that I made the right choice, however, because I don't think anyone needs me to tell them that vampires and werewolves are all inherently gay—symbolically if not also literally.

I hope that I've done a good job representing how integral they are to queer horror culture and its roots while also leaving them entirely off my recommendations list. They're important, but it was more important to me that I shine a light on other kinds of transformation arcs—especially ones made for those of us with depraved cinematic tastes who would otherwise get left out of the conversation. I'd love to turn that conversation one final time to the plot of *Martyrs*.

The film concludes with Mademoiselle, who is supposed to unveil this information that the organization has gone to such extremes to obtain. Rather than share Anna's revelation with the others, Mademoiselle kills herself. Her final words are "keep doubting."

Does she want them to keep doubting because to doubt is to be free of a terrible truth? Is doubting the entire point of what we do? Is the organization perhaps approaching some horrendous justice for all the pain they've inflicted? Would the absence of punishment be somehow worse? This woman has been responsible for countless atrocities and finally knows the truth about what is waiting for her. Is she trying to save her cohorts by taking the secret to her grave, or does she wish to condemn them further?

These were the sorts of questions that lingered in my mind from the first time I watched the film. I think that the act of leaving them unanswered makes this extreme cinema a piece of art.

They also add another layer to the traditional transformation arc that I found quite poignant.

Perhaps we can't handle seeing the truth until we have embraced the transformation required to discover it. Undoubtedly there is power in witnessing such truth, and that is how the film defines a true martyr: a witness.

I believe this power, this transcendent foresight into the very fabric of reality is extreme horror's conclusion to the transformation arc in the absence of a vampiric virus or a full moon. The change can be harrowing, but there is something indescribable waiting on the other side for those who survive.

AMERICAN
MARY
(2012)
BDSM,
BODYMODDING,
AND BABES IN
BLACK LEATHER

"I don't think it's fair that God gets
to choose what we look like on
the outside, do you?"

—Ruby, *American Mary*

Vital Statistics

Directed by Jen and Sylvia Soska
Written by Jen and Sylvia Soska
Cinematography by Brian Pearson
Edited by Bruce MacKinnon
Starring Katharine Isabelle as Mary Mason, Antonio Cupo as
Billy Barker, Tristan Risk as Beatress, and Paula Lindberg as Ruby
2012, Canada, 102 min.

There is a certain look that a lot of queer horror had in the 70s and 80s that was reflective of gay clubs, and that is often associated with BDSM. Chains. Piercings. Black leather. Instruments of torture. It was very prominent to see this in horror movies, especially in vampire films. (There are some really, really kinky vampire movies that came out of the 70s that I elected not to touch on, but that I was shocked made it past censors.)

If you're a fan of the genre, there's probably one movie in particular that comes to mind when I describe this aesthetic: Clive Barker's 1987 film *Hellraiser*. *Hellraiser* was adapted from his novella *The Hellbound Heart*, which is about a man who gets so bored of earthly pleasures that he summons otherworldly creatures in order to experience deeper sensation. It's my favorite horror book, and I think the movie was a surprisingly accurate adaptation of ethereal themes that must have been challenging to put to film.

Hellraiser is not only the pinnacle of that aesthetic, which I'd hoped to include with at least one of these recommendations, but it also has an ongoing legacy of queer themes. Lechmarchand's box (known in the film canon as The Lament Configuration) has that transformative element built in. The iconic cenobites are depicted as otherworldly angels who exist outside of our binary concept of gender—a point that was hit quite heavily with Jamie Clayton's depiction of The Hell Priest in the 2022 Hulu remake. Frank's journey of experiencing everything has interesting parallels to classic queer cinema's recurring theme of seductive corruption, and Julia has that recurring obsessive quality that we see in horror's most ambiguous characters.

Honestly, I wanted to include *Hellraiser* more than just about anything. Unfortunately, it's just too perfect of a queer movie to put on a list of lesser known queer films. It's so queer, and it's so blatant about it, and everyone already knows that it was created by a gay man. I just didn't feel like I had enough new things to say about it to justify the idea of it being underrepresented within the community. I almost included Barker's lesser loved 2008 film *The Midnight Meat Train* instead because it also has strong queer themes, but again, of course it did. Clive Barker is possibly the most prolific and profound queer author of our time. All of his work is going to be that way.

If I couldn't get that classic queer atmosphere by talking about *Hellraiser* or its creator, it seemed only right to include a movie that was directly inspired by Barker's work. *Hellraiser*'s inclusion of body modification inspired the Soska Sisters to center a story within that niche of the subculture to wonderful effect.

It is worth noting that Jen and Slyvia Soska have attracted a fair amount of controversy in the years following *American Mary* for their handling of actresses on set, as well as some of their unsavory industry connections. Many fans have been concerned about the incestuous implications of both of their cameos across their work and their exaggerated personalities when presenting television as themselves.

I wanted to acknowledge these things because they are more recent than some of the controversies that have come up about other creators previously mentioned in this book, and maybe more relevant. I also ask you to bear in mind that this essay is about the art, not the artists. It is not my intention to condone or handwave any bad behavior, but I also don't believe that the creators are the most interesting part of this movie, which addresses several underrepresented elements of queer experiences.

American Mary takes influence from the iconic bondage aesthetic, but it also does a lot with queer themes and nuance. There's the sort of *Frankenstein*-esque element that asks whether a creator or the creation is more monstrous. There's the sense of empathy for someone who has been cast out. It also offers something queer audiences are always asking for: found family. The film is too singular to be entirely set aside, and I'd like to focus on the parts I think make it worth remembering.

The film follows bright medical student Mary Mason, who is struggling to stay afloat financially. After she is assaulted by her professor, she drops out of school and uses her knowledge of anatomy to make ends meet in the world of body modification. She performs increasingly extreme alterations on her clients while also coming into the sort of powerful position needed to get her revenge.

An aspect that I really appreciate about the film is how it's Mary's "normal" life that causes the most harm. While trying to carve out a living for herself, she is objectified, pushed toward sex work that she feels uncomfortable with, exploited, and eventually assaulted by the person she had looked up to the most. It isn't until she falls in with the more marginalized bodymodding community that she is properly valued.

Initially she does seem pressured into performing this work, and there are moments early on of doubt and revulsion. But ultimately, at least in my reading of the film, she learns to embrace those in our society who are different and feel gratitude toward them for embracing her. It's the bodymodding community that values her for her mind, her skills, and her ambition once she has settled in. They create a safety net for her within their ranks when she has nothing else. She's able to rise to fame in this world because of its preexisting sense of close connection to one another.

I also have to take a moment to praise a couple of the individual characters. Mary's introduction into this whole world is through Beatress, a woman who is in the process of transforming herself to look like a real-life Betty Boop through cosmetic surgery. It would have been incredibly easy for her to become a laughingstock because the concept of her character sounds ridiculous—especially when we meet her through Mary's early, cynical eyes. (A small complaint that I have about the movie is how Mary never truly appreciates what a good friend she has found in Beatress.)

Beatress is one of my favorite modern horror characters, because she's just so sweet and empathetic and accepting of everyone. She's a great example of queer resistance through joy because she lives her most authentic self so unapologetically that it's honestly infectious. I think most people in the queer community have their own Beatress as well—someone doing the underappreciated work of building networks and introducing the people who feel most isolated into the groups that might understand them. It's a queer archetype that we instantly recognize, but that feels underexplored in the horror genre.

Another character that we don't see many equivalents of is Ruby. She is one of the only asexual horror characters that I can think of by name, and while her relationship to her sexual identity is not indicative of the wider asexual experience, it is portrayed in its own right as something positive and fulfilling to her. "A doll can be naked and never feel shy or sexualized or degraded. That's what I want."

Although Mary doesn't take the request seriously at first, Ruby's reason for wanting a modification was so impactful for me. I had never seen such a singular relationship to one's body and desires discussed so explicitly and with so much passion in film. Ruby's husband is less understanding, and his violent reaction to his wife's modifications acts as a catalyst for the movie's finale where he ultimately murders Mary. Some viewers criticized the film for saying that it was her involvement with this community that led to her downfall, and not, you know, her violent and illegal revenge against her professor. I personally feel like the opposite is true: it's not her involvement with this community that hurts her, it's "normal" society's violent reaction to what they don't understand.

American Mary is not perfect in its representations, nor is it above criticism as a queer allegory. Mary herself can be quite judgemental at various points in the film, and she is repeatedly sexualized in a way I felt was unnecessary to and sometimes detracting from the plot. And of course there's harm in the recurring narrative that individuals are pushed into their alternative lifestyles exclusively by trauma.

There's also an uncomfortable implication running underneath the narrative that these sorts of fringe communities will widely give passes to other sorts of taboo behavior. I was never fully comfortable with the notion that making out with your twin is the same level of freak as having your tongue split or dermal implants put in.

American Mary is the sort of movie that I encourage viewers to engage with critically, but I do encourage engagement with. It excels in so many aspects such as paying homage to classic queer cinema, depicting underrepresented subcultures, and indulging in tragic but endearing character work. It also works as just a violent, twisted film of revenge, which is always one of my favorite types of horror.

THE PERFECTION
(2018) 
REVISITING A FAVORITE

"You have been, and always will be, the person who makes my heart skip a beat when you play."

—Lizzie, *The Perfection*

Vital Statistics

Directed by Richard Shepard
Written by Richard Shepard, Eric Charmelo, and Nicole Snyder
Cinematography by Vanja Černjul
Edited by David Dean
Starring Allison Williams as Charlotte, Logan Browning as Lizzie, and Steven Weber as Anton
2018, USA, 90 min.

spoke in my *Martyrs* chapter about some of my previous efforts to highlight queer horror movies, and how my essay "Witness: The Transformative Power of *Martyrs*" was my first nonfiction work to make it into print. Before that, however, I had the honor of being in Dread Central's 2022 Pride lineup with an article called "*The Perfection*: A Love Letter to Lesbian Horror."

It was fascinating to go back and read that article after doing so much of the work for this book because while my horror preferences haven't really changed, my understanding of queer cinema has evolved dramatically. I was certainly onto something in that article, but it feels like I almost stumbled onto those revelations by chance because I lacked so much context and appreciation for the culture's historical roots at the time that I wrote it.

The Perfection is not subtle in its sapphic themes, but it was built on the back of horror that had to be. There was the golden age of sapphic vampires that I've alluded to, but even that representation was conditional on the idea that the lesbians got punished for their evil ways at the end of the story. *The Perfection* feels radical not only for depicting human lesbians in their full glory, but for letting them have a happy ending.

I also love how the film plays with our understanding of queer-coded language in classic horror cinema. The ideas of obsession, protection, and competition are all present and twisted within the film's presentation of its main couple. Watching the film for the first time, I felt like it was toying with me and my expectations. After revisiting my article and rewatching the film in preparation to cover the topic again, I realize just how masterfully it drew from those previous depictions of queer characters.

The story follows Charlotte, a former cello prodigy who had to quit a residency at one of the most prestigious music academies in the world to go home and take care of her sick mother. After her mother passes, she seeks out the new star student, Lizzie.

Their chemistry is instant and undeniable, but is also set up like a classic film rivalry. Charlotte, who has had to put her career on the back burner, has every reason to be envious of this young, bright, internationally renowned musician who has essentially replaced her. At this point I was certainly expecting one of the women to be evil, and for the horror to come from one targeting the other. This expectation is reinforced with how suspiciously willing Lizzie is to accept Charlotte back into the fold, and into her bed.

The setup seems to be for a virus movie. Many people mention a sickness in the background of establishing scenes, and Lizzie becomes very sick the day after the two hook up. She gets violently ill on the bus after the two decide to spend Lizzie's break traveling together, and they're both kicked off in the middle of nowhere after she throws up. In her feverish state she believes she's seeing bugs crawling underneath the surface of her skin, at which point Charlotte convinces her to cut off her hand.

When the narrative backtracks, we see just how deeply Charlotte had manipulated her in that moment. The sickness was due to drugs Charlotte had been slipping her, the bugs and virus mere suggestions that she had planted before putting the cleaver into Lizzie's hands. Lizzie has returned to the music academy missing her hand and unable to continue with her craft. The owner of the academy, Anton, is getting ready to kick her out of her residency as she is no longer able to play, despite the fact she has given her life to his teachings and has nowhere else to go.

Lizzie, seemingly in a mad state, drives back to the academy with Charlotte in the trunk of her car, demanding Anton's help in getting violent revenge against the woman who took everything from her.

The movie backs up a final time to reveal another big twist: the women are collaborating with one another. Charlotte's motivation in taking Lizzie's hand was not jealousy, it was protection. Having grown up in the academy as one of many students who were abused and assaulted by Anton, Charlotte had hoped to protect Lizzie from his treatment by severing her one connection to him. She promised to be there to support Lizzie, and she upholds her promise by helping her stage her own kidnapping. This gets them through the doors of the academy so they can enact their joint revenge.

While Anton and his fellow abusive teachers torment the long-lost Charlotte as a distraction, Lizzie spikes their drinks and separates them from one another so that they can be picked off.

The Perfection has echoes of the movies that I've chosen up to this point. The sense of rivalry that Mrs. de Winter feels with Rebecca is reflected here in the early act as the two women engage in what can only be described as instrumental foreplay upon the stage. The second act backstabbing and conspiracy recall the convoluted and intimate murder scheme in *Les Diaboliques*. The constant revelation of new information and toying with traditional narrative structure felt like it took a page out of the psychological horror presented in *Martyrs*. These are just a few examples, but the parallels to previous sapphic horror films feel almost endless.

What I love best about *The Perfection* is the ending, which was actually the focus in my previous coverage of the movie. By the time they have taken their bloody revenge and the women are reunited, Charlotte has also lost a hand in the fight for survival. This has left both women missing a piece of themselves and unable to make the music that has essentially shaped their entire lives and served as the foundation of their relationship.

The movie ends with them teaming up one final time in an unexpected and indescribably poetic fashion: to play together. The women share a performance seat, both straddling the cello, and Lizzie does the fingering while Charlotte works the bow across the strings. It's not only a striking visual of unity for the two and how they complete one another, but a perfectly happy end for our pair of antiheroes.

The Perfection has no shortage of trauma, loss, and pain. But it's also a rare expression of queer joy and a rare narrative where everything more or less works out. It's an absolute roller coaster through the ups and downs of sapphic horror tropes, but also a triumphant love story with an end like no other.

This is my all-time favorite lesbian romance onscreen, and my appreciation for it has only deepened over the course of this project.

X
(2021)
TI IT'S
A ALL
DISCO

"I think that it would be easy to make her one-dimensional, either stupid or mean or something like that."

—Brittany Snow

Vital Statistics

Directed by Ti West
Written by Ti West
Cinematography by Eliot Rockett
Edited by David Kashevaroff and Ti West
Starring Mia Goth as Maxine/Pearl, Jenna Ortega as Lorraine,
Brittany Snow as Bobby-Lynne, Martin Henderson as Wayne,
and Scott Mescudi as RJ
2021, USA, 106 min.

n my last chapter I spoke about how doing the research for this project, filling gaps in my own knowledge, and immersing myself in classic queer horror for a while helped further inform my deep appreciation for the modern examples of queer horror. There have also been instances where some of my hottest takes have cooled off since I outlined this project. While it's certainly made pulling quotes easier now that more people are talking about queer themes in movies like *Hausu* and *Possession*, sometimes I've wondered if some of my job here isn't being done for me.

One thing that has kept me focused and motivated throughout has been that however much attention these films get in the queer community, they deserve more attention. This title in particular is being entirely slept on.

X was a sleeper hit of a movie. The trailers were underwhelming and though Ti West had a record of making solid films, he certainly wasn't the big name that he is today. Competition was also fierce at that time, because horror fans were eating well in 2021. *The Black Phone* was an overwhelming success, Nia DaCosta gave us an epic continuation of *Candyman*, and everyone was hyped up to finally be getting *Halloween Kills*. And that was just the big-budget titles. Streaming gave us masterpieces like *Jakob's Wife*, *Mad God*, and one of my personal favorites from the year, *The Sadness*. The horror market was so blessed that on the day *X* released, it wasn't even the movie I was most excited for that day. (I only happened to catch it on release because I was already at the theater for *Umma*, a fact I find absolutely hilarious in retrospect.)

At this point in the book, you're probably familiar enough with my film preferences to understand why *X* works so well for me. Ti West did a great job recapturing that grimy 70s grindhouse feel, which works as a loving homage to one of my favorite eras of horror. The avant garde editing, in stark contrast, felt more modern and polished—reminiscent of the 2000s New French Extremity movement, my other favorite era of horror. This, combined with excellent performances, surprisingly emotional plotlines, and a score so iconic I play it every day in my office, and this film feels like it was just made for me. It even has some of my random favorite things to see in horror like a former ballerina who snaps, an unexpected gator kill, and of course, full-frontal male nudity.

I absolutely adore *X*, and I'm one of the few people who still prefers it to the instantly iconic followup, *Pearl*. I have some unkind thoughts about the third and final installment of the trilogy, *Maxxxine*, but even that has done little to tarnish my love of *X*, which is currently sitting as my second-favorite film of all time. We're not talking about it just because I love it, though; we're talking about it because it was astoundingly queer.

2023 saw my most recent addition to the canon of queer horror essays in the form of another piece for Dread Central entitled "It's All Disco: Bobby-Lynne, Pearl, and Queer Representation in *X*." It's one of the articles that I'm most proud of over the course of my career, and was actually the sample of writing I sent in to accompany my pitch of *Queer Tastes*. It didn't get the attention that I was hoping for, however.

Part of the issue was my timing. I sent this in to Dread Central during the one year they didn't have a Pride article spotlight, and it ended up being published in August, after Pride Month festivities had largely ended. Part of the issue was Ti West's timing. Though *X* had originally been conceived of as a single film, quarantine regulations in Australia where it was filmed gave him the idea to shoot a second movie on the set that they had built. *Pearl* was envisioned before filming on *X* even began, and green-lit shortly after, allowing the movies to be released in the same year. Fans truly responded to *Pearl*, however, and even in my attempt to pull focus back to the original movie, it seemed like fans had just moved on.

I'm here to share those thoughts about *X* again, and once more sing the praises of my favorite pansexual character in horror media: Bobby-Lynne Parker.

Though the movie goes back to the days of the 1970s grindhouse slasher, it has done away with some of the worst, slut-shaming tropes that were present in stories of the day. The plot sees a group of adult filmmakers renting out a farmhouse where they plan to shoot the first high-quality porno. The elderly couple that owns the farm kills them off one by one to satisfy the wife's urges now that her husband's heart is too weak to give her the physical attention she craves. From the perspectives of both the killers and victims, sex is portrayed largely as a good thing—something we don't see often in the genre.

In a movie that equates the thrill of murder to sexual gratification, a lot of questions are opened up about our main killer Pearl's preferences. We know she doesn't like blondes, but she seems rather indiscriminate when it comes to gender. In fact, she actually claims that the star of the film, Maxine, is the one she wants out of the group. Since the last victim held captive in the basement was a man, this presents Pearl as bisexual—metaphorically, if not strictly in practice.

We see her portrayed in *X* as someone who wants a thrill from individuals that catch her eye, and we know she can get that feeling from both men and women. This is rather analogous to the experience of bisexuality, which is defined as being attracted to two or more genders. It's an experience that I don't see tackled often in media, especially horror media where the token gay characters often go out of their way to express their sexuality. What fascinated me even more than the bisexual metaphor presented in Pearl's character was the strong impression that our stripper-turned-porn star Bobby-Lynne Parker is pansexual.

A lot of people consider the differences between bi and pan to be semantic, especially as there is so much overlap. While bisexuals are attracted to two or more genders, pansexuals (such as myself) experience attraction to anyone completely outside of their relationship to gender. Perhaps it's a stretch to call Bobby-Lynne canonically pansexual in a film that shows us experiences, rather than bogging itself down with labels. What I can claim with confidence is that I was drawn to her immediately because I had never seen my relationship with my own sexual identity summed up in a horror film so succinctly: "Everybody likes sex. It's a gas. We're just not afraid to admit it. Queer, straight, Black, white—it's all disco."

Cutting through the Southern slang and expressions of the time, this quote says a lot about Bobby-Lynne as a character. She's honest, confident, and above all, accepting. Her sexuality is an integral part of her that she never tries to hide, but she also never tries to label it, either. Even though the term "pansexual" defines a very specific subsection of the queer community, those of us who identify as pan share a common struggle with such boxes. It's more about the feelings and experiences than it is about categorization. In this way, I saw a lot of myself portrayed in Bobby-Lynne, regardless of how she would self-identify with all the terminology available to us in the present-day lexicon of queerness.

She has another quote later on that pinpoints perfectly the most deep-rooted source of fear in the movie. While it resonated because it came from her in particular, it also touched on one of the biggest themes of the story as a whole: "One day, we're gonna be too old to fuck. And life's too short if you ask me."

This is the heart of emotion in *X*. The things we want aren't going to last forever. Whether it's fame, experience, or pleasure that you're seeking, life is just too damn short. Bobby-Lynne dies young and pretty, but a major point of the movie is Pearl feeling like she's outlived her desirability. What happens to us when we've gotten to an age where we can no longer chase the things we desire? One of the worst fates imaginable is living long enough to feel trapped with your regrets.

This is manifested in the characters differently, but it's something they all have in common. Maxine plans to escape this curse by becoming famous and being immortalized in the movies. Church-going Lorraine, encouraged by Bobby-Lynne, plans to take the opportunity to get onscreen with the others so she can break out of her shell. Pearl, who already feels her best days are behind her, turns to her more violent desires in an attempt to ease that fear of having missed out.

It's Bobby-Lynne who goes to her grave with the fewest regrets. She never gets her American dream house with a pool to sun what the good lord gave her, but she does live every day honestly. She knows who she is and what she wants. Even her on-again-off-again relationship with her male costar Jackson is not a connection that she seems dissatisfied with. There is a lot to be said about taking what you want from life experiences, rather than trying to fit into someone else's idea of what you should be. Where a traditional horror movie would paint her as the dumb blonde or the whore archetype, *X* gives us someone who is charming, considerate, and open-minded. Bobby-Lynne Parker is the pansexual icon.

There is also a lot of comfort in Pearl's narrative, even though the audience is set up to root against her. One thing West accomplishes in this film is to give us a sympathetic villain. You don't have to condone Pearl's murders to feel the catharsis that she experiences from their execution. While she may not be a great source of life lessons, she does set a good example in some ways. She found a partner who understands and embraces the parts of her that can't be satisfied within the heteronormative confines of traditional marriage.

Then, she takes matters into her own hands when she begins to feel neglected by that partner. She teaches us that it's never too late to reconnect to a part of ourselves if it's a part that we still long for. In that way, I'd argue that Pearl is also a queer horror icon.

It is not often I find a horror movie that so deeply expresses nuances of sexual identity in such a casual way. *X* is able to present different facets of my lived experience of sex-positivity outside of gender confines through its killers and its victims without ever preaching—that's nothing short of a miracle in my eyes.

It is still so important to tell queer stories in no uncertain terms. We need more horror movies where these topics and labels are discussed and featured front and center because representation is vital. Audiences need characters that show them they're not alone. However, it is films like *X* that will tide us over, films that can be interpreted and identified on an individual level. We relish films that are messy and emotional, where sexuality and morality are ill-defined themes to make of what you will. I hope we see more of its kind alongside films that are more blatant in their approach to queer storytelling.

HUESERA:
THE BONE
WOMAN
(2022)

BLESSED
WITH
ANOTHER
ICON

"It was very important to portray the kinds of women who had been through this breaking down process and that they had found ways to reconstruct themselves."

—Michelle Garza Cervera

Vital Statistics

Directed by Michelle Garza Cervera
Written by Michelle Garza Cervera and Abia Castillo
Cinematography by Nur Rubio Sherwell
Edited by Adriana Martinez
Starring Natalia Solián as Valeria, Alfonso Dosal as Raul,
Mercedes Hernández as Isabel, and Mayra Batalla as Octavia
2022, Mexico/Peru, 97 min.

Coming fresh off the idea that we need both subtle and blatant queer representation in horror media, I think it's worth mentioning that the blatant representation will never resonate as well for me.

I mentioned this in the last chapter, but identifying as pansexual has involved a lot of inner turmoil with my own labels. Not only was it incredibly hard to settle on a term within the community that resonated, I stumbled right into an ongoing controversy. Pansexuals and bisexuals have such overlapping communities and ways of identifying that my very existence as pansexual sometimes feels semantic. Historically, many in the community said that having a term this specific helps participate in bisexual erasure, or enforce the common misconception that bisexuals are transphobic. The idea here is that if someone believes bisexuals are only attracted to men and women, they are intentionally excluding nonbinary and trans people. To reiterate: the accepted definition of bisexuality is someone who is attracted to two or more genders, and this is inclusive of trans people.

Virtually every pansexual I know is happy to just not engage in this kind of discourse—especially online where it's still more pervasive. The experience and terminology of this type of attraction are both fluid and nuanced. We're getting to a place, especially at in-person Pride events, where people can be more flippant about why they chose a specific term. I know a lot of bi/pan people who fall so strongly into both definitions that they will use both labels, or just choose based on which flag they feel has better colors. I'm glad to see this shift, and to see more pan flags at Pride events in the last handful of years, but I carry some of the unease of past discourse with me.

Struggling to find a label, and then years of struggling to defend that label, have primed me to have a deeper appreciation of representation that focuses more on experience than on terminology. While it leaves certain facets of what we see up to interpretation, it also feels more authentic and sincere to me.

I think it's so positive to have horror movies with proud queer stereotypes finally getting a chance to shine, and to have movies that get into the weeds about labels. To have a character proudly say "I'm gay" or "I'm bisexual" or "I'm a lesbian" is a privilege, and I'm grateful for it. At the same time, I find that I never feel as deeply about movies where the sexuality of characters is laid out with such certainty.

What I like about Michelle Garza Cervera's directorial debut *Huesera: The Bone Woman* is that it can avoid those conversations and labels while also being very blatant in its bisexual/pansexual themes.

The film follows Valeria as she tries to prepare for her first child with her husband Raul. A large part of the story's focus is on the bone-creature that Valeria is seeing in and around the nursery that she's putting together, and on her unease with her own changing body throughout the course of her pregnancy. She tries to rid herself of a curse that she thinks is putting her and the baby at risk, which involves partaking in a dangerous ritual to clear her of evil spirits.

While the ritual is ultimately successful, Valeria learns to prioritize herself anyway. She goes through hell to protect the baby, but ends up leaving the baby to be raised alone by Raul, since motherhood was never something she wanted for herself.

After all of this, she goes to live the life she did envision for herself, and that she spoke of often and at length with her former girlfriend Octavia. (It's unclear at the end of the movie if she is going on her own, or if she plans to meet up with Octavia, though I hardly think that this changes the impact of the ending or its inherent queerness one way or the other.)

I have seen this described many times as a truly feminist piece of horror. I agree, as it not only shows the terror of a changing body during pregnancy, but has clear messaging of women being more fulfilled by nonmaternal priorities. It presents Valeria as a good person who is still able to prioritize herself. It shows surviving as something that goes hand in hand with learning to appreciate one's sense of self. Obviously these are all incredible feminist messages.

One aspect that I wish had been centered more in the conversation about the film, however, is Valeria's sexual identity. *Huesera* resonated with my experience not just as a woman, but specifically as a pansexual woman. Valeria loved Octavia, but I think she also must have loved Raul deeply, despite the sort of traditional, heternormative life that he represents for her over the course of the film. It was only by experiencing deep feelings for him that she allowed herself to get lost in his vision of what their future together should look like. As a queer woman who is, again, in a straight-passing relationship, I found myself deeply moved by Valeria's loss of connection to her identity, and metaphorically, her queerness.

My participation in my relationship makes it inherently queer, but I consider myself lucky to be in a situation where I have strong, ever-present connections to the queer community who remind me of that fact. I remember, from times when this was not always the case, how easy it can be to lose yourself. Even now, it is a constant struggle to remind myself that my relationship does not need to be measured in traditional, straight milestones. If I didn't have that community, and my voice, and my experience navigating this space, I wonder how easy it would be to lose myself in a man's idea of the traditional family unit.

The movie also tricked me by playing on my preconceived notions of traditional horror narratives. Watching Valeria fight so hard to save the life of her unborn child taught me to view motherhood as the upcoming reward for her struggles, and I honestly wasn't expecting her to walk away from it. Getting through all the trials of the movie successfully and still watching her choose to honor herself in the end of all things was such a gift.

I identify with her character because the story is not spelled out, and I have no doubt that my own preferences and experience color my read on this movie. I know many people in the community had a much harsher view of her story, which they perceived to be more about a lesbian pressured back into the closet. This makes her family seem more cruel, Raul seem almost villainous, and Valeria herself seem weaker—not to mention that it makes the ambiguity of the ending feel more ominous. In a version of the narrative where Octavia is a metaphor for Valeria's true self, then anything short of seeing them together feels dissatisfying. I think that may well be a contributing factor to why the initial hype about this movie faded relatively quickly, despite strong critical reception.

I obviously don't like this version of the story as much. It feels darker, but also less realistic and nuanced. It also would rob me of some sorely needed badass bisexual representation and thrust a subplot of shame onto Valeria that I don't think is founded in what we see onscreen. This is not to say that my version is correct, or better. I'm sure that if I were a closeted lesbian who was terrified of imminent motherhood, I would find far more comfort in seeing those aspects of my life reflected in Valeria as well. I bring it up because I think this is the beauty of ambiguity in cinema. It leaves room to be reflective of the viewer.

There was such a long period of time where not using labels was the only way that queer stories could get told. I think that now the avoidance of labels can make stories more universal, without them feeling as though they are hiding their queer nature. *Huesera: The Bone Woman* does this brilliantly. No matter how you interpret the fact that Valeria is queer, there is no denying that she is. The vagueness allows us to project parts of ourselves onto her and her story, without ever denying or obscuring the fact that she is one of us.

I don't think I will ever get tired of this kind of queer narrative, nor will I ever stop seeking them out. It is exceptional, almost decadent, to have such explicit queerness that is still up for interpretation. It is made even better by the fact that queerness is a feature of this narrative, and not the conflict.

SKINAMARINK (2022)

QUEER GRIEF AND QUEER JOY

"Can we watch something happy now?"
—Kevin, *Skinamarink*

Vital Statistics

Directed by Kyle Edward Ball
Written by Kyle Edward Ball
Cinematography by Jamie McRae
Edited by Kyle Edward Ball
Starring Lucas Paul as Kevin, Dali Rose Tetreault as Kaylee,
Ross Paul as Father, and Jaime Hill as Mother
2022, Canada, 100 min.

have more movies from the 2020s than I do from any other decade, despite the fact that at the time of editing the 2020s are barely half over. When whittling down my selections I tried to be the most selective of movies from the last five years, because this is an era of film that I felt was well-represented in the book already.

Thanks to a more positive cultural shift in favor of the LGBTQIA+ community, however, we are just now entering a time where there are so many queer stories that representation is falling through the cracks. Instead of beating myself up about how many films I was choosing from each year, I decided just to spotlight some of the most interesting trends I've noticed in the queer media that I feel aren't talked about enough.

One such topic is the intertwined nature of grief and joy. A complaint that I see often is that movies—horror movies in particular—too often focus on queer trauma. I do think that there is a need for more stories depicting queer joy, though I think horror leans toward trauma for the straights as well just by the very nature of the genre. I am certainly not helping with my recommendations in this book because I gravitate toward the sort of horror that collects content warnings. There have been a couple of lighter picks, such as *Hausu* and *The Return of the Texas Chainsaw Massacre*, but generally I seek catharsis through grief-centered narratives.

Other people might prefer some of the flamboyant horror films, such as *The Rocky Horror Picture Show*. There is such a demand for this that whenever there's even a slightly queer horror movie that's more fun than tragic, it gets embraced quickly and whole-heartedly by the community. Movies like *Jennifer's Body*, *Freaky*, and to some extent even *Sissy*, all reached easy cult status within the community for their snappy one-liners and use of color.

I think it's interesting, though, that some of the most radical joy for queer horror fans has come out of some of the darkest horror films.

This recommendation is about Kyle Edward Ball's experimental horror film *Skinamarink*, which I promise we will get to. The movie warranted some very strong mixed reactions and also some of the queer community's funniest moments. To understand all that, however, we've got to go back to 2014, to Jennifer Kent's directorial debut, *The Babadook*.

The Babadook is a harrowing allegory for depression that is deeply uncomfortable to watch despite its uniquely unsettling visuals. It follows a struggling single mother, Amelia, and her son Samuel whose persistent belief in monsters is alienating them from school, family, and other children. It's about grief and isolation and the very real monsters that we must learn to live with.

It became an instant meme when Netflix accidentally put it in the "LGBT" category of the streaming service back in 2017. The idea of the Babadook being a queer icon was manufactured after the movie, but was persistent. I was just starting my career in horror journalism around that time, and let me tell you, it was absolutely insane to have to cover the ongoing Tumblr controversy where bisexuals were offended that the rest of the community (and allies) were claiming that the B in LGBT stood for Babadook.

That aspect smoothed over rather quickly, and the Babadook remained, against all odds, a part of our community. We had essentially stolen him. A lot of Babadook merch was sold in Pride colors, with rainbow flags, and it wasn't terribly uncommon to see a couple of fully costumed Babadooks at events and marches.

It was the sort of unhinged marketing moment that has proven impossible to recreate, even for more intentionally queer movies.

Part of it is that the LGBTQIA+ community is very active online. Tumblr in particular bred this sort of absurdist, referential humor that made Netflix's initial mistake spread like wildfire on the platform. Once something is embraced into the Tumblr canon, the users are very likely to dig their heels in—and part of the fun for many people was the sort of in-joke that it should have been obvious *The Babadook* was always queer.

I think there was another, hidden aspect to the longevity of this joke, however. Before the Netflix slip-up, *The Babadook* wasn't particularly geared toward queer audiences. It was well received by horror fans, critics, and indie circles, but it wasn't a huge name initially. Even when it hit streaming, it lacked the blatant representation, romantic subplots, and coloristic stylings that would have drawn queer horror outlets to spotlight the film.

Practically overnight, queer fans were swarming to this movie, and while the memes may have pressured them to like or pretend to like it no matter what, I think many must have genuinely found something in the story that resonated with them. As I mentioned earlier, it's not a comfortable watch. But the idea of having something hidden, something attached to you that you cannot defeat or escape from, and even the idea of living with a persistent secret, all brush against themes that we've seen depicted over and over in queer horror. Whether we like to admit it or not, I think the queer community is generally more receptive to stories about grief and trauma than non-marginalized communities.

The Babadook may have been a funny outlier, but we can see that situation reverse-engineered when we look at the queer community's response to *Skinamarink*.

Skinamarink is a low-dialogue experimental film that thrives on its lack of plot and heightened sense of surrealism. It follows two children trapped in a house with no doors or windows. The rooms are always poorly lit, the video is grainy, and the shots are always set up in such a way that despite the claustrophobic setting, there's a sense of openness, as though something could be lingering just outside our field of vision in any direction.

The movie was, to put it simply, divisive.

During its very limited theatrical run, my viewing experience summed up the two most popular reactions to the movie. The man to the right of me had a cardiac event because he was so scared. The man to the left of me demanded a refund because it "wasn't even a movie." A lot of people in our screening, whether through fear or boredom, didn't make it to the credits.

The genius, or stupidity, of *Skinamarink* is that it doesn't show you things to be afraid of. It creates an atmosphere where you are meant to experience your own most primal fears, creating a nightmarish landscape that you don't fully understand and where anything can happen.

I was still covering horror movies full-time at this point in my career, and I noticed that a lot of the loudest fans in the horror community were proud to have not understood the *Skinamarink* hype. Many had fun dogpiling on this viral movie moment that they thought people were hyping up for no good reason. (I am not exempt from this, because there is nothing I love more than the hilarity of a one-star *Skinamarink* review.)

The queer community was having an entirely different conversation about the movie, however. Many of my friends who were deeply impacted by the film felt that it tapped into something from their own childhoods—and I'm assuming that none of them were ever trapped for days in a house with no doors or windows. I genuinely believe that it was easy for them to project their own fears and experiences onto this otherwise very surreal nightmare canvas because queer people do have a stronger sense of empathy for stories about trauma. The ideas of being misunderstood, abandoned, isolated, and left alone to confront demons in a house where you feel trapped are probably easy to trace back to the experiences of many queer children who grow up without a support system.

I won't go so far as to say that *Skinamarink*, intentionally or otherwise, is a queer allegory. I will say that its atmospheric, vague sense of mounting dread seemed to resonate most strongly in communities that had preexisting, communal trauma to unpack.

We saw the completion of the reverse Babadook arc at the end of 2022 when the Fisher-Price toy phone featured in the movie became a staple at Pride events. It was one of the most recognizable props featured in *Skinamarink* (which sorely lacked for other recognizable imagery outside of grainy blue photo filters), and suddenly it was showing up bedazzled as a purse, made into patches, and just carried as an accessory for queer fans who inexplicably felt that *Skinamarink* was our next big moment.

We're a few years out and already the *Skinamarink* phone, while still a less-circulating meme, has all but entirely fallen out of fashion in person. It didn't have the staying power of *The Babadook*, perhaps, but I do think it's interesting to see another viral, seemingly unrelated piece of queer iconography spring up from an absolutely downer horror film about trauma.

Skinamarink is actually my least favorite film out of the twenty that I recommend in this book. I find it a fascinating study in experimental horror, but I personally found Kyle Edward Ball's short film work to be infinitely more affecting. The entertainment value here has been watching audience reactions more than in considering the movie itself. However, it is a title that I recommend everyone watch once, fully immersed. No lights, no phones, no distractions (and ideally without the man beside you having a cardiac event, which was quite immersion breaking). You might hate it, or you might love it, or perhaps like myself you might just find a deeper understanding of the conversation that surrounded this very singular release.

If nothing else, I think that watching *Skinamarink* offers a better understanding into the very specific wavelength that the queer community sometimes gets on. Seeing that phone pop up as a silly, viral shout-out to a controversial horror movie was so indicative of the way that we express our joy, even in the context of our darkest moments.

SCREAM
(2022)
THEY CAN
NEVER TAKE
THIS MOMENT
AWAY FROM ME

"One thing that I love about Mindy is that she's queer. She's a queer woman of color like myself, our first openly out, queer character in the *Scream* universe, but her personality isn't her sexuality."

—Jasmin Savoy Brown

Vital Statistics

Directed by Matt Bettinelli-Olpin
Written by James Vanderbilt and Guy Busick
Cinematography by Brett Jutkiewicz
Edited by Michael Aller
Starring Neve Campbell as Sydney, Courtney Cox as Gale,
David Arquette as Dewey, Jasmin Savoy Brown as Mindy,
Melissa Barrera as Sam
2022, USA, 114 min.

'm not sure there is a feeling more universal than having a favorite character who is ruined by the writers. I mean, what do writers really know anyway? Between Flanderization of characters, changes in creative visions, burnout, and executive interference, there is an entire minefield of ways that a favorite character can be absolutely assassinated. This is a more common problem in long-running television series and books than it is for movies, but any time that characters are reused across multiple installations of a story, you run the risk of seeing them twisted into a version of themselves that you don't recognize.

The one good thing about having little representation is that you don't have to feel the pain of disagreeing so strongly with the actions of one of your favorite characters. The bad thing, of course, about getting more representation is that you run the risk of going all in on a character who lets you down later on.

This essay is about Mindy Meeks-Martin.

I am writing this in the winter of 2025. I obviously don't know what the state of the *Scream* franchise will be by the time the book is released or by the time you, the reader, find it. To say that it's in a tumultuous state currently would be an understatement. So let's not talk about anything past *Scream VI*.

As a matter of fact, let's also put a pin in talking about *Scream VI*. It's going to come up, believe me, but for right now let's just do what I'm here to do and make a recommendation.

As a queer person, I fully endorse the fifth installment into the *Scream* franchise, which to my annoyance is just titled *Scream*. (I personally refer to this entry as *5cream* so much that it's painful for me to type it any other way. In an interview I did with Radio Silence Productions, the creators of the film, they also referred to their movie as *5cream* and said it was popular to do so on set. This isn't relevant to my point, I just wanted to share.)

Scream follows the town of Woodsboro and a new group of teens that is being attacked by a new, more vicious Ghostface-masked killer. This draws the attention of the previous survivors, Sydney, Gale, and Dewey, who come to teach the next generation how to make it through a slasher movie where everyone is a suspect.

Mindy, one of the targeted teens, is paper-perfect representation as far as I'm concerned. Her inclusion in *Scream* was everything that I ever wanted in my queer horror characters.

She is smart, funny, and beautiful, and she is clearly a lesbian without the studio trying to make a big deal about the fact that she's a lesbian. She was portrayed by Jasmin Savoy Brown, who is an incredibly talented actress actively involved in the queer community. She's also well known for playing young Taissa in *Yellowjackets*, which is another example of excellent lesbian representation onscreen.

She's also a woman of color, which means that this is not just queer representation, but intersectional queer representation—something that I support, even if I am clearly not the most qualified to speak on it. The cherry on top for me is that Mindy is the niece of my all-time favorite *Scream* character, Randy Meeks.

Randy was a diehard horror fan who lived and breathed the movie tropes, so of course I had always related to him very strongly. To see him remembered in the legacy of the franchise, and being brought back to life in a way through Mindy, was very gratifying. Brown did an excellent job with the character, and absolutely stole the show.

Her relationship to her sexual identity felt very casual in *Scream*, and though some fans wanted more, I think it was perfectly in character for her to have bigger things on her mind as a masked killer picks off all her friends. The inclusion of an (actually) confirmed queer character in the franchise was something I found interesting, and I assumed they'd have plenty of time to explore later down the line. (This was back when it seemed like the torch was going to be passed along to this new, younger cast of characters for the rest of the series.)

So, now it's time to take that pin out of *Scream VI* and make some Scream fans really mad at me.

I hated *Scream VI*.

I don't think it worked as a *Scream* movie or as a standalone film, and it's the hardest one of the series for me to sit through. Given the uncertain future of the franchise, I find it heartwarming that a majority of fans got to end on what they considered a high note. The audience score is currently over 90% on Rotten Tomatoes, years out from its initial release. I know many people who said it was their favorite sequel, and even a couple who thought it surpassed the original 1996 film.

For me, *Scream VI* felt like a parody of itself, more akin to a *Stab* movie than a *Scream* movie. It follows the "Core Four" to college in New York, where they are trying to forget about their traumatic high school experience while being targeted by a Ghostface-worshipping family of psychos.

The premise is fine, but the body count was a little low for my tastes. I was bothered that almost as many Ghostfaces die on-screen as their other victims combined. While it's not outside the scope of the franchise to mock its own killers, pushing it to this extent felt almost as though it was mocking the audience. The message of family togetherness felt a little cheesy after it failed to build a real sense of tension for the main characters, and sometimes it felt like a trailer for a version of *Scream 7* that, after poor handling from the studio, fans will never get.[8] The makers of

---

8. The current version of *Scream 7*, which (as of editing this article in 2026) is slated to come out this year, has had to take an entirely different direction after firing its lead actress, Melissa Barrera. Several fans of the franchise, myself included, had already planned to boycott be-

Scream VI felt unable, or unwilling, to make any bold changes to the status quo; this felt like a huge backslide from the attitude in the previous film, which meant business.

My main problem, however, was the fan service. They wanted this to be the *Scream 2* of the new trilogy. But while *Scream 2* offered timely commentary of movie trends in the 1990s, *Scream VI* offered mostly cheap references to *Scream 2*. Mindy, who had been my favorite character just a movie before, became the person whose job it was to point out "hey, this is just like what my Uncle Randy said!"

This felt like a radical, practically overnight Flanderization of what had been an interesting and relatable character. The salt in the wound was that her survival in the film felt unearned. Despite a constant, running commentary of paranoia, Mindy only survives by dumb luck and Ghostface's inability to stab with any kind of accuracy. Not a single one of the Core Four was ever in significant danger over the course of this film—even her brother Chad, who survives several worse-but-apparently-not-fatal stabs to the spine.

One final point to this is that one of the shockingly few characters who we do lose is Mindy's girlfriend, meaning that *Scream VI* wanders right into the pitfall of the "bury your gays" trope, which I honestly believed had fallen out of fashion by this point in horror.

I could go on for a long time about elements of *Scream VI* that didn't work for me, but believe it or not I am mostly here to talk about Mindy. It sucks anyway not enjoying a movie that other people seem to love en masse—and it really sucks being mildly offended by what feels like an utter failure of previously good representation.

---

fore the studio's string of controversial marketing decisions, including advertising partnerships with both AI and gambling companies. I said I wasn't going to talk about *Scream 7* but every day since writing this essay I feel more appalled by the direction they've taken, and more nostalgic for a time when this franchise mattered.

But you know what?

They can never take *Scream* (2022) Mindy away from me.

I can be annoyed all day at how they chose to portray her in *Scream VI*, offended by her girlfriend being one of only a few to die, and nihilistic about the hope of the franchise ever producing another movie I'd be willing to watch in a theater. But I still got that moment of joy when I was in the movie theater to watch *Scream* return after ten years, and I got a cute moment of a badass, movie-loving lady, curled up on the couch with her girlfriend.

I have done my best to achieve a lot of things with this project. I wanted to analyze movies that made an impact, that got overlooked, that started conversations. I wanted to memorialize moments in the community before they can be lost to time. I wanted to introduce you, hopefully, to one or two queer icons in horror movies that you hadn't met or considered. But I do those things because I know how important it is to find surprising little moments of joy, and to see snippets of yourself on the big screen.

Mindy Meeks-Martin was, briefly, one of those sweet moments for me. I don't agree with how the next movie treated her, and even less with the direction that the franchise seems to be taking. But I know that Mindy is still important representation to many, and I'm glad that they still get to see themselves in her. It's why I'm genuinely pleased that so many people did like *Scream VI*.

I SAW THE
TV GLOW
(2024) 
THE MOVIE
THAT WOULD
HAVE CRACKED
MY EGG

"Sometimes *The Pink Opaque* feels more real than real life."

—Maddy, *I Saw the TV Glow*

Vital Statistics

Directed by Jane Schoenbrun
Written by Jane Schoenbrun
Cinematography by Eric K. Yue
Edited by Sofi Marshall
Starring Justice Smith as Owen, Jack Haven as Maddy,
Helena Howard as Isabel, and Lindsey Jordan as Tara
USA, 2024, 100 min.

This has been a very personal project. That's how all projects are when you're talking about media that has mattered to you—especially once identity comes into it. I have done my best to cover themes that I've noticed are relevant to the community at large, but I am still only one small part of the community. I've tried to be inclusive in these essays by encouraging readers to think for themselves about what points do and don't matter to them, what tropes and visuals do and don't reflect their own experience, and offering popular counterpoints to my interpretation of things.

That doesn't change the fact that queer, for me, is largely about sexuality and preference as opposed to gender identity. I can talk about the history of trans representation, how certain pieces of media have opened up my eyes to larger issues, and how controversial depictions have sparked interesting conversations with members of the trans community.

It is rare, however, that a piece of media makes me reflect on my own concept of gender. Womanhood is something that for a long time I didn't need to define. I just took it for granted that it was part of my experience because I had never felt any kind of gender dysphoria to tell me otherwise.

Then I watched Jane Schoenbrun's film *I Saw the TV Glow*.

The story primarily follows Owen, an outcast child in 1996 who gets pulled into an obsession with a kids' TV show called *The Pink Opaque*. His friend Maddy, who introduces him to the show, is also obsessed with it until she goes missing.

When she returns, years later, she says that everything Owen has ever known has been a hallucination. They are in fact the characters Tara and Isabel from *The Pink Opaque*, and have been buried alive by the show's villain. She suggests their entire world is just a hallucination as they run out of oxygen, and that only by being buried alive again can they hope to return home to live as themselves.

Owen does not take her up on her request to be buried alive, and he never sees her again. His asthma worsens as he grows up, often leaving him struggling for air. When he goes to revisit the show, it's not at all like he remembered. "What if she was right? What if I was someone else? Someone beautiful and powerful? Buried alive and suffocating to death on the other side of a television screen?"

As I said in the chapter on *Perfect Blue*, the shedding of a safe identity is a traditionally queer arc. The presentation in *I Saw the TV Glow* felt particularly reminiscent of other trans-specific allegories such as *The Matrix*, which is more explicit about the sheltered, safe life not being real.

There is the choosing to live in a comfortable reality, or the danger of stepping into something unknown. There's also the element that choosing one means losing the other for good. Owen loses the idea of seeing himself as the woman in *The Pink Opaque* to keep living in the life he has always known, rather than gamble his life to become the person that on some level he always saw himself as. The tragedy and uncertainty of that decision haunts him, up to his implied, inevitable death.

After its wide release on Shudder, *I Saw the TV Glow* became a sort of litmus test. There were people who thought it was slow and that it took its incomprehensible themes too seriously. Others—largely made up of the trans community—saw themselves reflected so obviously in the movie that it became their favorite of the year. A few people I know even credited the film as helping them to embrace their gender identity.

I am at a point in my life where I have more trans, gender-fluid, and enby friends than I have cis friends, so it's not like I never think about gender. Part of being in a queer space—or any empathy-focused space, really—is trying your best to understand the lived experiences of other people.

For a long time I've believed that my gender-nonconforming associates feel a deeper connection to their chosen gender than I feel to being a woman. Sometimes it has made me wonder if I am a woman at all or if I am a woman out of convenience. Given my habitual struggle with labels, the idea of gender being such a personal and impactful part of self-identifying was honestly just too daunting to think about. It took me 20+ years to identify as pan because language feels so finite compared to the boundlessness of self-expression. Committing to a single word felt overwhelming and impossible.

After seeing so many people share that this movie had made them question their identities, or tipped them off to the fact that they were trans (often referred to in the trans community as "cracking their egg"), I decided that maybe it was time to ask those questions about myself.

The thing about gender is, as I said earlier, that it's a concept so full of nuance that it's difficult to fully grasp. It's a social construct. As society shifts, the definitions and confines of gender inevitably shift as well. This is one of the things that makes it so hard to have eloquent debates about it in today's political climate: the lack of clear definition.

I am more confident in my blind spots, however, than I was before I took the time to explore such an idea. I have a better understanding of the role that gender has played in society traditionally. I have a better concept of what gender means to me— that it is nothing but the social framework in which we prefer to be viewed. I feel more assured in the idea that I fit, as an individual, within the category of woman. I'm getting more comfortable with the idea of discomfort over definitions. Looking inward, and doing the work to find myself, was infinitely rewarding.

I encourage all of my fellow cisgender people to ask yourself about your identity as well. Go on that journey. Even if it scares you. Especially if it scares you. There is a certain sort of built-in comfort in being cis where society doesn't challenge your gender, but you'll never get stronger if you're not challenged. Thinking about those sorts of big picture concepts is a great way to feel more comfortable in your own skin, even if nothing changes. This is a big reason why reflecting on the things we see in movies can be so impactful.

While I couldn't relate to being raised as a boy and seeing myself in a female character on TV, I could relate to Owen—and especially Maddy—in just how much love for a show can matter. I also idolized 1990s female characters and took strength from seeing bits of myself in them. Channeling my energy into watching and rewatching *Buffy* and *Xena* as a kid got me through the tough things in my life. Both of those shows probably influenced my perception of what a woman is.

I can't say that I'm one of those people whose egg was cracked by watching *I Saw the TV Glow*. But. This is one of those movies that forced me to sit down and have a difficult conversation with myself about who I am and how I see the world. The fact that it addresses something so personal in a way so many people identified with was nothing short of magical. The fact that even in-universe it does this by addressing how important it is for queer kids to see themselves represented in media? Well, that, I think, makes it the perfect final recommendation for a book that has been all about queer representation.

CONCLUSION

MY YEAR
STUDYING
QUEER
HORROR

want to thank everyone who has come along on this journey with me.

When I first pitched *Queer Tastes*, I had ten controversial movie recommendations, years of online discourse, and a dream. Unpopular queer representation in horror is something I've felt passionately about for the last several years. There is a huge difference, however, between writing stray articles on a topic and dedicating a year to immersing yourself in that same topic. And what a year it's been.

Not only have I rounded out my list of recommendations, I had to pare it way down just to make it manageable. Alexandre Aja's 2003 film *Haute Tension* was one of the first movies I picked, as it has long been a problematic favorite of mine. I was ready from the start to pull out all the stops in justifying its inclusion, only to realize I didn't need to. I found an increasing number of people willing to look back on the title charitably, and even a few willing to embrace the questionable sapphic element of it favorably.

Julia Ducournau's 2021 film *Titane* was another one that I cut from my original roster. I found it to be a conversation-worthy piece of transgressive body horror despite the fact that many in the community found it offensive. The dozens of lengthy reviews tearing into it made up the first rabbit hole I really fell into for this project, before I decided that there were just other titles that better represented my own journey with gender exploration.

I didn't even get the chance to talk about some of the queer themes from more recent titles that piqued my interest, such as

Yorgos Lanthimos's *Poor Things* (and that one could have really riled some people up because it's one of those rare adaptations that I actually prefer to its source material).

I also spent about two months just wading through classic horror collections looking for more pre-70s hidden gems. There were so many excellent titles that felt like gold when I found them that I didn't even get to write proper essays on because of the abundance of options I'd collected by the time I finished. There wasn't room for the awkward but hilarious representation in William Byron Hillman's 1982 film *Double Exposure*, or my interpretation of the flamboyant performance of Ray Dannis in T. L. P. Swicegood's 1966 gem of a film, *The Undertaker and His Pals*. Even knowing full well that I wasn't going to include any vampire movies on my final list, there were a handful of research days that I spent catching up on as many as I could, just so I could have a more complete picture of lesbian horror cinema.

There were so many podcasts and reviews and op-eds that I consumed for this project that informed my experience despite not even making it into the footnotes. Shudder ended up being a wealth of polished quotes and reputable sources, but I barely scratched the surface of what I got from there either. I had to rein myself in more and more because I was falling down a new rabbit hole every week and my word count was beginning to swell, even as I was decreasing my total number of recommendations.

I've felt so blessed to have this opportunity to delve into queer horror history, and especially at this point in time. Being a queer person in America feels more unsafe today than it has at any other point in my lifetime. I have gay and lesbian friends whose marriages are in jeopardy of no longer being legally recognized. I have trans and nonbinary friends who are losing their fights to get gender-affirming care. I know so many people who are having to have serious conversations every single day about where it is and is not safe for them just to exist—let alone express themselves authentically.

Working on a research project of this nature has simultaneously been a great distraction from the terrors of the world and a great reminder to engage more with my community. It's become increasingly apparent to me why representation is so important and why we can't afford to forfeit all the progress that we've fought so hard for.

The last year has been terrifying, but it has also been filled with so much joy.

Getting more informed and becoming more comfortable with my voice in this space has led to some fantastic opportunities. I've audited more classes, attended more Pride events, and met more of my queer icons in this last year than in the entire rest of my life. Even despite the constant wave of bad news, I feel like I've seen more hope and understanding and camaraderie out in the wild than I would have imagined possible.

In my introduction I invited readers to come along and see these twenty movies with me. What you didn't get to see was how working on a nonfiction project that I feel so passionately about has given me the opportunity to learn something new nearly every day that I've been writing this book. Words cannot fully express how rewarding the experience has been. In parting, I'd like to invite you to do one more thing.

Find twenty movies of your own. Find fifty. Find a hundred. Develop so many hot takes that they wouldn't all fit in a book together. Get as passionate as you possibly can about movies or television or books or music or whatever it is that makes it easier to wake up to a scary world every day. Be inspired to learn and evolve and seek connection to your community.

To all the allies and to the queer readers in particular, I encourage you to keep going. Let the fictional horrors drown out the very real nightmares for a while if you're able. We're all tired, and we need the rest, but we've got to keep going. The world needs more queer voices.

FULL WATCHLIST

This list covers not only the twenty films I recommend, but the full list of movies referenced.

Rebecca (1940)
Nosferatu (1922)
Les Diaboliques (1955)
The Haunting (1963)
The Haunting of Hill House (2018)
The Texas Chain Saw Massacre (1974)
Psycho (1960)
Saw (2004)
Hostel (2005)
Final Destination (2000)
Suspiria (1977)
Suspiria (2018)
Hausu (1977)
Ringu (1995)
Ju-on (2002)
Audition (1999)
Possession (1981)
Frankenstein (1931)
Deadly Games (1982)
Scream (1996)
Rope (1948)
The Toxic Avenger (1984)
The Rocky Horror Picture Show (1975)
The Toxic Avenger (2023)
The Silence of the Lambs (1991)
Hannibal (TV series, 2013–2015)

The Return of the Texas Chainsaw Massacre (1994)
House of 1000 Corpses (2003)
The Devil's Rejects (2005)
A Nightmare on Elm Street 2: Freddy's Revenge (1985)
Perfect Blue (1997)
Black Swan (2010)
Requiem for a Dream (2000)
Martyrs (2008)
Ginger Snaps (2000)
The Hunger (1983)
Queer for Fear (2022)
American Mary (2013)
Hellraiser (1987)
Hellraiser (2022)
The Midnight Meat Train (2008)
The Perfection (2018)
X (2021)
The Black Phone (2021)
Candyman (2021)
Halloween Kills (2021)
Jakob's Wife (2021)
Mad God (2021)
The Sadness (2021)
Umma (2021)
Pearl (2021)
Maxxxine (2024)
Huesera: The Bone Woman (2022)
Skinamarink (2022)
The Babadook (2014)
Jennifer's Body (2009)
Freaky (2020)
Sissy (2022)
Scream (2022)
I Saw the TV Glow (2024)

ABOUT THE AUTHOR

Cat Voleur is a full-time horror author with such titles as *Revenge Arc*, *The Lorekeeper*, and *My Apologies to Tanya Grace*. She is a member of the International Association of Media Tie-in Writers and a co-host of *The Nic F'n Woo Cage Cast*. When she's not creating or consuming morbid content, you can find her relaxing with her small army of rescued felines.